# WHY PEOPLE HATE COPS

## AND WHAT COPS CAN DO ABOUT IT

KEITH POUNDS

Why People Hate Cops
And What Cops Can Do About It
All Rights Reserved.
Copyright © 2020 Keith Pounds
v1.0

The opinions expressed in this manuscript are solely the opinions of the author and do not represent the opinions or thoughts of the publisher. The author has represented and warranted full ownership and/or legal right to publish all the materials in this book.

This book may not be reproduced, transmitted, or stored in whole or in part by any means, including graphic, electronic, or mechanical without the express written consent of the publisher except in the case of brief quotations embodied in critical articles and reviews.

Pounds Publishing

ISBN: 978-0-578-22660-6

PRINTED IN THE UNITED STATES OF AMERICA

Other Works by Keith Pounds

A Concise Encyclopedia of the Choctaw Indians: Past and Present, *Infinity Publishing* (2002)

The Psychology of Management: Different Ways on Different Days, *iUniverse Publishing* (2008)

You're Hysterical: How Feminine Hysteria has Eliminated the Male Role in Modern Society, *Infinity Publishing* (2011)

# Table of Contents

PREFACE ..................................................................... i

HISTORY .................................................................... 1

FALSE ALLEGATIONS AND CORRUPTION ....................... 7

PROFESSIONAL BIAS ................................................. 15

CIVILIAN PSYCHOLOGY .............................................. 35

COMMUNITY POLICING .............................................. 48

POLICE CANINES ...................................................... 57

SOME REALLY WEIRD STUFF ....................................... 70

POLICE MILITARIZATION ............................................ 86

PTSD AND LAW ENFORCEMENT ................................... 95

SOME STEREOTYPES...ACCURATE AND INACCURATE... 116

SOME FINAL THOUGHTS ............................................ 140

# PREFACE

> *"Every normal man must be tempted, at times, to spit on his hands, hoist the black flag and begin to slit throats"*
> – H.L. Mencken, American journalist, essayist,
> satirist, cultural critic (1880 – 1956) –

Having served as a U.S. Navy hospital corpsman across the globe during the Lebanon-Grenada era, I learned as a young man the importance of studying historical data and how a review of that data could be used to analyze past and current targets, tactics and procedures.

From my earliest days at the (then) Naval School of Health Sciences in San Diego, California, I became fascinated with the history of combat injuries and how commanders have dealt with their dead and wounded, in the present and in the past.

My studies would later be framed by historians like Victor Davis Hanson – author of *The Western Way of War* – which detailed how the ancient Greeks formed the impetus of what would become modern warfare, as well as *The Face of Battle* – by renowned author and English military historian John Keegan – which challenged many of the myths we had about combat, including the effectiveness of certain weapons and troop formations.

Those early studies as a junior enlisted corpsman included reviewing historical battle injury data to evaluate battlefield survival. The study of the combat environment and how it involved an array of unpredictable factors, to me, was fascinating.

Things like types of injury, area(s) affected, supplies available, availability of evacuation, but also things like weather and time of day (or night) painted a picture of how difficult the duties of a combat medic could be.

As a small sample, during the Vietnam War, "survivable deaths" – deaths of which the patients should have survived with proper care – could be blamed on three specific injuries. Those injuries included blood loss (60%), tension pneumothorax (33%) and airway obstruction (7%).

Another example would be that with improved logistics and casualty evacuation – as well as improved medical training for our troops – the U.S. military reduced overall combat fatality rates from 19.1 percent in WWII down to 15.8 percent in the Vietnam War and further to about 10 percent currently.

While these are fascinating examples of our technological advances in combat medicine, it's shocking to realize that even today the leading causes of combat-related injuries remain blood loss, tension pneumothorax and airway obstruction.

An even more inspiring example includes a 2011 study in the *Journal of the American Medical Association* which reviewed early casualties among the 75th Ranger Regiment in Afghanistan and Iraq prior to 2010. It found that the regiment's rates of 10.7 percent killed in action and 1.7 percent who died of wounds were lower than the broader Department of Defense overall rates of 16.4 percent and 5.8 percent, respectively.

The 75th Regiment's improvement in casualty rates was attributed to newly implemented Tactical Combat Casualty Care training which provided better pre-hospital care by non-medical personnel.

Survivability is critical to winning. That's precisely why our military has went to such great lengths to ensure it.

It shouldn't at all be surprising to know that we can do the same with law enforcement data. We have loads of it! A central problem though will be the unwillingness to objectively review it all.

This book will attempt to do that, reviewing available data so that both law enforcement and civilians can get an outside (military) view of how complex the work is, and how complex civilian interactions with law enforcement can be. Of course, law enforcement knows much about this already.

To be clear, law enforcement already has the data it needs to address crime the way we want them to address it, but we'll look at how the media is preventing our cops from doing that!

Why then, a law enforcement officer may ask, do so many in the general public hate cops? Much of the answer lies in our current legal system – particularly that involving the long-lost war on drugs – which has been forced upon far too many otherwise law-abiding citizens. These unfortunate folks have had far too many instances where they've had to interact with law enforcement when there was no other reason for them to do so.

Lastly, I'm sure this book will challenge many myths that both law enforcement and civilians have about each other.

I hope I've put this work together in a way that we can all understand the many sides of our debate and discussions about both the effectiveness and inadequacies of the law enforcement profession.

# HISTORY

*"Go sir, gallop and don't forget that the world was made in six days! You can ask me for anything you like, except time!"*
— Napoleon —

At a September 2017 lecture for The Heritage Foundation, William J. Bratton - former NYPD Commissioner - gave his thoughts on "policing" in America. He explained how policing throughout the 20th century and into the 21st century has continued to change in fundamental ways.

In his words, policing has "swung like a pendulum from prevention to response and back to prevention." He makes an interesting point if we consider that so much of the public today (unfortunately) views law enforcement through the lens of Jim Crow-type glasses, if not thoughts centered on the police as being violent members of our society.

Few would argue that law enforcement has an embarrassing history of enforcing unjust laws against the public it has sworn to protect and serve. With that terrible history, it is not irrational to suggest that the concept of "ethics" may indeed be a relatively new one for the law enforcement profession. That said, the evolution of law enforcement in America tells an interesting story.

Law enforcement was virtually non-existent in colonial America. Exceptions would include a local "Justice of the Peace" who might serve warrants, etc. Actual "policing" though was conducted through what could be labeled as "social shame." Law enforcement officers were simply not necessary as individual communities relied on their own customs and traditions as benchmarks for behavior.

An Italian area of town had certain cultural norms that were easily enforced by social shame. A different area of Irish residents had different social norms that community members relied on to judge and influence behavior. A local drunk was easily identified by the community, and that drunk was shunned by community members.

> *As law enforcement agencies grew, individual officers no longer really knew everyone in the neighborhood on a "first name basis" and community members no longer had close relationships with their respective "beat cop."*

As areas grew though, communities previously separated by cultural and ethnic identity came into closer contact with each other. As such, a more organized way to enforce behaviors was needed. We can fairly say that this "melting pot" is at least one of the major reasons why a professional, dedicated police force became important, in order to address crime uniformly and to maintain order.

In these earliest days of policing in America, the familiar "beat cop" became an important symbol of law enforcement in each community within larger cities. In smaller towns, there was the "town cop."

As he personally knew everyone in the neighborhood, it was easy for him to help the homeless find something to eat, make sure local kids were in school, and even occasionally help folks find a job. These officers were very often able to anticipate – and even prevent – crime by influencing behavior. As he was such a recognizable figure in the neighborhood, it was easy for him to enforce community expectations,

And yes, sometimes by force.

In the "New Deal" era of the 1930s, government agencies ballooned in hopes to address the needs of children, the homeless, housing, and even employment. As that address of "social ills" was in a real sense taken off the backs of law enforcement, policing was beginning to focus more on the "response" to crime.

As law enforcement agencies grew, individual officers no longer really knew everyone in the neighborhood on a "first name basis" and community members no longer had close relationships with their respective "beat cop." For the sake of argument, we can fairly point to this era as being a time when American citizens first began to view "the police" as not so much "officer friendly," but as a threatening force.

America's civil rights era of the 1960's had much to do with changing the face of law enforcement. By this time, American law enforcement activities had wholly moved from crime "prevention" back to crime "response." With patrol cars – and eventually the 9-1-1 system – law enforcement no longer helped to prevent crime. Officers mostly showed up after crime had happened.

Patrol cars allowed officers to cover more area, but simultaneously created a perceived barrier between law enforcement and the public, as opposed to earlier, more personal "cops walking the beat." Even more, law enforcement officers showed up in their patrol cars "after the fact," dealt with issues, then retreated to the safety of their patrol cars – again separated from the public – so they could wait for another call.

As cities grew, areas with little to no crime seldom saw law enforcement officers. In other areas - most prominently in minority communities, where there was lots of crime - law enforcement was a constant presence, most often with bad consequences.

For a short while, criminal behavior was blamed on things like poverty and socioeconomic status. Fortunately, studies convinced us that these things were not at all primary predictors of criminal behavior. Although, the introduction of the "Broken Windows Theory" suggested that things like prostitution, graffiti and loitering were predictors of crime in an area.

As such, law enforcement officers began once again addressing some of the "social ills" in society. This gave birth to the very recent concept of "community policing." Tragically, the recurring "budget cuts" in the early 2000's prevented many departments from adequately addressing those problems.

At about the same time, the growing use of personal cell phone videos posted on social media sites did much to severely damaged the image of law enforcement. While the news media was responsible for over-dramatizing many police-civilian interactions, the fact is that the public saw a lot of bad cops doing bad things, a lot.

Today, coming full circle, many departments are attempting to regain some semblance of a "beat cop" mentality, implementing "community policing" policies which encourage officers to participate in community programs. We can often see officers participate in school and church programs, and even exhibit some of their equipment and local fairs and festivals. Larger departments even have specialized units organized for that specific purpose.

Still, in the same departments, policies and procedures – intentionally or not – encourage actual "patrol officers" to keep their distance from the public and remain non-confrontational, which is best done in their patrol vehicles.

> *Effective community policing efforts quickly lose their gains once the public meets many rank-and-file officers on the street.*

This is at odds with much of the "community policing" efforts today. We see many departments implementing programs in schools, churches and local festivities, but much of the public views these as temporary, site-specific functions to get media attention (we'll explain in later chapters how the media has been law enforcement's biggest enemy).

The public knows that the actual behavior of today's rank-and-file patrol officer is far-removed from what is displayed during fairs and festival exhibits. As a case in point, consider meeting a local law enforcement officer on the sidewalk in your town. If you were to say, "good morning, officer," he or she is very likely to nod their head and probably even offer a "good morning" in return. Although, if we are honest with ourselves, we are very unlikely that that officer will initiate the greeting.

In the almost overwhelming number of cases, you will not get a greeting from a law enforcement officer in today's America unless you offer it first. That's just simply the truth, and we all know it. Effective community policing efforts quickly lose their gains once the public meets many rank-and-file officers on the street. This is a major reason why so much of the public is uncomfortable with law enforcement officers.

For some reason, law enforcement hasn't been able to clean up this aspect of its image, and it's one of the major variables that have helped to create anti-cop sentiments. Sadly, it's been partially created by the hands of cops themselves.

We could make even a brief history of policing in America much more detailed than what we reviewed above, but even in this short chapter the reader can see how law enforcement itself has had to evolve with the times, whether due to political pressure, or the media, or other forces.

On one hand, law enforcement today draws a much greater spotlight than it ever has. And the profession should be credited with how it is showing the public its commitment to ethical applications of the law.

As we'll review further in this book, our law enforcement officers today face not only a hostile media, but the challenges of dealing with international terrorism, domestic terrorism, gangs, gun violence, homelessness and the opioid crisis, all on top of what we would consider "routine" policing (which itself could keep an officer on his or her toes for an entire shift).

Still, the recurring outline in any discussion of law enforcement today seems to be based on a single question: Is the role of law enforcement today one of preventing crime or the measurement of how law enforcement responds to it? The search for answers will be prevalent throughout this book as we examine how different agencies have addressed those two questions.

In addition, we will ask why it is that in the very areas where community policing is the most visible, crime rates are the highest. How is that possible if community policing efforts are said to help reduce crime?

Even Dr. Chuck Russo – Program Director of Criminal Justice at American Military University – at least partially agrees. In A February 2016 piece for the university's website *In Public Safety*, entitled "The evolution of police: From the 19th century beat cop to today," he recognizes that, "Unfortunately, many citizens today consider police to be a necessary evil rather than assets who protect and assist those in their community."

A February 2017 *USA Today* piece entitled "When policing stats do more harm than good" insisted that, "When cops are under pressure to show productivity, they make stops and hand out summonses they may not otherwise." As it further noted, "This creates excesses that don't actually reduce crime."

My point in highlighting these two pieces is that we don't need to look far to see how law enforcement officers – and their departments – can, as the *USA Today* piece suggests, create "a wedge between the police and the communities they are supposed to serve."

# FALSE ALLEGATIONS AND CORRUPTION

*"Some rise by sin, and some by virtue fall"*
*– Escalus in "Measure for Measure" –*

## Racial Hoaxes

In June 2018, Khalil Cavil, a 20-year-old waiter at the Saltgrass Outpost restaurant in Odessa, Texas – who is reportedly of mixed black and white heritage – posted on his Facebook page a receipt from one of his tables scrawled with the words "We don't tip terrorists."

As Cavil wrote, "I share this because I want people to understand that this racism, and this hatred exists." He added, "Although, this is nothing new… it is still something that will test your faith."

Cavil's employer banned the customer from the restaurant and followers on Facebook even sent Cavil money. Ultimately, it was discovered that Cavil fabricated the note himself. In early July, it was determined to be a hoax, and that Cavil wrote those words on the receipt himself.

Also in June, a waitress at another Texas restaurant blamed police for writing a note targeting Mexicans. She too later admitted that she wrote the note.

In September 2018, a New York woman claimed teenagers yelled racial slurs at her and left a racist note on her vehicle. Police later determined she made up the whole thing. Again in September, LGBTQ Ohio University Student Senate member Anna Ayers reported that she found "hateful, harassing" messages referencing her LGBTQ identity at her desk. The next Monday she added that she received further messages threatening her life. A few weeks later she was arrested and charged with three counts of making a false claim.

In mid-November 2018, Goucher College in Towson, Maryland – on the outskirts of Baltimore – witnessed several instances of racist graffiti, including the spray painting of the word "Nigger," the letters "KKK" and swastika graffiti targeting black and Latino students. Also in November 2018, a number of "racist notes" were slid under the dorm room doors of Kissie Ram and several other African American students at Drake University.

> "... The number of hate crime hoaxes actually exceeds the number of convictions. The majority of these high-profile incidents never happened."

By early December 18-year-old Ram was issued a summons for "making a false report to law enforcement." She later admitted being responsible for the notes. In the same month, several racist notes found at Drake University were determined to have actually been written by one of the students who claimed to have been the target of one of the notes.

In January 2019, Native American activist Nathan Phillips told media that white students from Covington Catholic School swarmed him and blocked him from leaving a Native American event he had attended. Video evidence later proved that Philipps actually confronted and harassed the students. The video also showed several members of Black Hebrew Israelites using racial and anti-gay slurs against the students.

And who can forget the months-long media frenzy in early 2019 over Jessie Smollet's staging a racist, anti-gay attack on himself?

Will Reilly – an African American associate professor at Kentucky State University – studied what appeared to be an increase in racial crimes in recent years. He ultimately published a book on his findings entitled "Hate crime hoax: How the Left is selling a fake race war." He found that the supposed increase in race crimes was largely due to an increase in hate crime hoaxes.

As Reilly wrote, "In major cases, almost all of them have been hoaxes. The number of hate crime hoaxes actually exceeds the number of convictions. The majority of these high-profile incidents never happened."

My point here is to call attention to the fact that people will lie! As the record clearly shows, they will definitely lie about matters involving race. I'm hopeful we will keep that in mind as we discuss "corruption."

## Body cameras

On July 4, 2019, a group of officers with the Tempe Police Department in Arizona were asked to move or leave a Starbucks because a customer felt "uncomfortable." (Note to self: Don't go to Starbucks again). Also in July, a Pennsylvania woman who falsely accused two police officers of rape was sentenced to 23 months in prison.

We could review an entire chapter on the introduction of body cameras (body cams) for law enforcement officers and the early – and ongoing – pros and cons of their use. A prominent point in the discussion though is that accusations of abuse or mistreatment by law enforcement officers quickly grabs the public's attention. And why not? Who wouldn't be deeply concerned to think that the law enforcement officers in their community were unfair and abusive? It's a legitimate concern.

Lucky for citizens in America, we have the 1st Amendment, the 4th Amendment's due process and a host of other protections that are not afforded to many people in the world. And we also have body cams!

Early demands were that law enforcement officers wear body cams so the public could actually see how abusive officers were. Indeed, one *Newsweek* study showed that having police wearing body cams "reduced the use of force by roughly 50 percent" and the instances of complaints against officers dropped by 90 percent.

The suggestion was that body cams have forced officers to be nice, and not so abusive. Of course, it could be equally argued that many suspects are less likely to be violent themselves if they know they'll be on camera, making it more difficult to claim mistreatment later.

Sure, body cams have caught some officers on video being abusive, but we've also seen just how much disrespect and abuse cops must put up with.

In the end, body cams clearly assist in police accountability and transparency, provide valuable evidence in court for both parties and help when investigating public complaints against an officer, especially in cases of police brutality and excessive force.

## Bad Cops

When a law enforcement officer abuses his or her power, commits a crime or makes a grave mistake, the recurring theme is that that officer was just a "bad apple," and that all cops hate bad apples. Unfortunately, there is sad, overwhelming, embarrassing evidence to argue that corruption, bad tempers and errors in judgment are rampant among law enforcement.

A June 2016, Bowling Green State University study – funded by the National Institute of Justice – found that between 2005 and 2011 some 6,724 cases of the arrests of law enforcement officers involved 5,545 officers. Averaging about 1,000 officers being arrested each year, the most frequent arrests were simple assault, driving under the influence and aggravated assault.

Forty one percent of the crimes occurred while the officers were on duty, and about 10 percent involved sex crimes. Mind you – as we would argue in regards to any other group – those numbers include only officers who were caught and arrested!

Some will remember that the country was rivetted in January 2018 with news that officers in Baltimore admitted that they carried "toy guns" to plant on people in case they accidentally shot an unarmed suspect.

In the same month, when four officers in Houston were shot during a SWAT raid, Houston Police Officers' Union President Joe Gamaldi chose a live press conference to threaten all the citizens of Houston who even voice an opinion about law enforcement. Very fortunately, all four of the officers survived, but rather than reserve his anger for actual criminals, Gamaldi shed light on what many fear is ingrained in law enforcement culture.

On live TV, he said;

> "If you're the ones that are out there spreading the rhetoric that police officers are the enemy, just know we've all got your number now, we're going to be keeping track of all of y'all, and we're going to make sure that we hold you accountable every time you stir the pot on our police officers."

Both of these incidents shocked much of the nation, but they are just two, very recent, examples of how law enforcement is very often its own worst enemy.

While these are national examples, any of us can sadly do a quick search of law enforcement corruption and misconduct and find dozens of recent cases in our very own state, and even communities.

To give just a few recent examples, in my own home state of South Carolina, in February 2019 a Sumter, SC police Sgt. was arrested for — and admitted to — "consensual oral and sexual intercourse with a woman at her home while he was on duty."

Also in February, a Sgt. with the Bluffton Police Department in SC was arrested because he "drunkenly assaulted fellow off-duty officers at a bowling alley and attempted to climb out of a patrol vehicle window."

In March, a corrections officer at South Carolina's Lieber Correctional Institution was charged with "misconduct in office, possession with intent to distribute marijuana, and introduction of contraband to inmates" after being arrested for using a state-issued vehicle to smuggle marijuana into the prison.

Also in March, several law enforcement officers from Orangeburg County, South Carolina and the nearby town of Springfield were charged with a variety of federal and drugs charges, including taking bribes in exchange for protecting drug shipments and committing visa fraud to help illegal immigrants stay in the country.

These cases were eerily similar to an April 2015 case when South Carolina's Lexington County Sheriff James R. Metts — who had been sheriff since 1972 and was the state's longest serving sheriff — received a sentence of one year and one day in prison for assisting illegal immigrants housed in the county jail to avoid federal authorities. The illegals were said to be the employees of a local Mexican restaurant chain owner who paid Metts bribes for his help.

Again in March, a Summerville, South Carolina police lieutenant was charged with first-degree burglary after allegedly breaking into a woman's home after she told him not to come to her home.

In April, South Carolina's Florence County Sheriff Kenney Boone was indicted on charges of embezzlement and misconduct for using county funds from a narcotics account to buy personal items. In the same month, an officer in Hardeeville, South Carolina was arrested for "using information obtained through his position as a law enforcement officer in the furtherance of aiding other persons to commit criminal acts." Authorities said they had been working a case involving prostitution and human trafficking, which led to the arrest.

The very next month, we discovered that the FBI was investigating several officers with South Carolina's Chester County Sheriff Department – including the sheriff – who had been indicted on federal charges of excessive use of force and conspiracy to cover up unlawful arrests, stemming from their being angry at a man for filming an arrest.

In June, an officer with the Landrum Police Department was arrested for misconduct and unlawful communication between October 1, 2016 and December 1, 2017. He was accused of "sending a photograph of his genitals to a woman, having sex with the woman on multiple occasions, and failing to respond to a call for service while having sex."

In the same month, off-duty Lexington County, South Carolina deputy Robert Scott – who had been a deputy since 1982 – was arrested and charged with driving under the influence of alcohol. He later resigned.

> It is time that law enforcement understands that when the public hears that these are "isolated incidents" involving "bad apples" it comes across as an insult, and it feeds the anger of those who distrust law enforcement.

In July 2019, a search for a suspect in Lexington County, South Carolina led deputies to the home of former Columbia, South Carolina Police Chief Randy Scott, who was charged with drug possession when meth was found in his bedroom. Scott had previously served not only as Columbia's Chief of Police but as a deputy in Richland County.

July was a busy month as we heard news of a widespread "ticket scheme" in Charleston, South Carolina. Officer Michael Baker admitted to fabricating traffic tickets in order to "boost" the number of tickets he was issuing. He resigned from the department and a second officer involved in the scheme resigned just weeks later.

These instances are shocking not only because they occurred within just a year's time, they all occurred within the same state, and involved both rank-and-file officers as well as country sheriffs. These instances occur at similar rates in every state and community in the nation, and the public knows it.

The public hears details about each and every one of these cases. It is time that law enforcement understands that when the public hears that these are "isolated incidents" involving "bad apples" it comes across as an insult, and it feeds the anger of those who already distrust law enforcement.

# PROFESSIONAL BIAS

> *"Why'd you come you knew you should have stayed*
> *I tried to warn you just to stay away*
> *And now they're outside ready to bust*
> *It looks like you might be one of us"*
> *— From the song "Heathens," by Twenty-One Pilots —*

## Job Stress

It's not difficult to find articles about the stress of serving as a law enforcement officer. While the list may be exhausting, we can quickly find many recurring themes among those writings.

Timothy Arouca – who holds the rank of Major in a large law enforcement agency in Florida – penned an enlightening October 2018 piece entitled, "The 10 worst things about being a police officer."

He acknowledges that being a cop comes with a "decent salary" as well as comfortable health and retirement benefits. Although, his list of "negatives" of the job might be eye-opening to some. I've listed them below in brief;

- **Excuses.** People tend to blame things on others, making even simple investigations frustrating for police.
- **Attitudes.** Even typically law-abiding citizens berate police over even simple traffic tickets.
- **The Hours.** Police work means "shift work." The long and irregular hours can be disruptive to personal and family time.
- **Stereotypes.** While television and movies may portray cops as "knuckle draggers," reality is that many are compassionate, caring people who truly want to help others.
- **Myths.** Too many people use television and movie perceptions to try to 'outsmart' the police to avoid arrest.
- **Perception of cop culture.** The idea that the 'thin blue line' concept creates a culture of corruption among law enforcement.
- **Scrutiny.** No secret that law enforcement officers are scrutinized more than most any other profession.
- **Politics.** Cops must often navigate the actual law and the (often incorrect) media and public perceptions of the law.
- **The Pain.** Cops must often deal with the pain and suffering of others.
- **Losing Peers.** Job fatality rates for law enforcement are disproportionately high.

A September 2016 piece in *Police One* magazine online entitled "5 stressors cops deal with that non-cops should know about" insists that after serving a few years in law enforcement, officers will find that the job "will change their outlook on the world, their interactions with others and in some cases their very ability to deal with others who are not in law enforcement. They will find that once close relationships with friends and family may fade."

We will discuss more about this very often acknowledged change among law enforcement officers in later chapters. For now, here is how the *Police One* article lists its choice of cop stressors;

- **Daily preparation for battle**. *Cops have bulletproof vests and guns for a reason; they stay ready for a fight.*
- **The cop attitude stays.** *The article suggests that the "cop attitude" can't be left at the office (We will also explore this much more in later chapters).*
- **Life in a fishbowl**. *Law enforcement officers are under constant scrutiny, even when off duty.*
- **Front row seat to despair.** *When cops show up, it is often because something bad just happened. So, many cops see bad things day after day.*
- **Riding the incident rollercoaster**. *On any given day, a cop can be eating lunch one minute, chasing a bad guy the next, then helping a severely injured child the next.*

In an August 2016 article in *Business Insider*, Ryan Wagner – assistant professor of Medicine at University of South Florida – wrote of what he called the "unique job stressors" of police work. Wagner's focus was on the "looming worry affect" among officers, and how that can affect officer performance and well-being.

He notes that while media portrayals may suggest otherwise, some studies show that mental health issues may not necessarily be higher among law enforcement officers compared with the general public. Interestingly though, he notes that officer deaths by suicides are in fact higher than officer deaths in the line of duty.

While Wagner does worry that officers often have repeated exposure to others' trauma – to which many attribute the symptoms of Post-traumatic stress disorder – he does remind us however that "stress inoculation training" offers a degree of "inoculation" to traumatic events or sights, and that training programs across the country are recognizing the benefit of such training.

He suggests that law enforcement stressors must also include inter-departmental politics as well as ongoing (and even increasing) media scrutiny. If we consider that, it may be wholly unfair to simply label law enforcement as being susceptible to PTSD, suicide or overall mental health issues because of work-related dangers. We must also admit that politicians, senior law enforcement administrators and the media may be equally (if not more) responsible. We will discuss this in much greater detail in our chapter *PTSD and Law Enforcement*.

While there is much to say about mental health issues among law enforcement, an equally important discussion can be made about the over-victimization of police work. And it is indeed rampant.

An April 2016 piece entitled "Why I hated being a cop" highlighted the thoughts of former North Charleston, SC police officer Raeford Davis, who spoke about his frustration in "combatting drug-fueled violence in minority communities."

Retiring from law enforcement in 2006, he began working with Law Enforcement Against Prohibition (LEAP), a nonprofit organization against the war on drugs. He speaks about his feelings of dissatisfaction in stopping kids in bad neighborhoods for simple drug possession, when he recognized that they very often had no other avenues readily available to them. He included one story about stopping an elderly black man simply for being in a bad neighborhood in a nice vehicle. Davis described how a police canine scratched the paint job of the gentleman's vehicle, then jumped inside and scratched the seats and interior.

## Police and Public Perceptions

The 2017 Pew Research "Behind the Badge" study helped to show just how far apart law enforcement and the public are in their perceptions of police work.

While the general public typically do not want more police officers in their neighborhoods, most police feel like more officers are needed. At the same time, majorities of both the police and the public generally view that the introduction of police body cameras has been beneficial.

When asked about police-involved shootings of blacks (and corresponding protests), most law enforcement officers viewed them as "isolated incidents," while most of the general public considered them something more. Interestingly though, when this area of the study is broken down into race, the numbers become a bit troubling.

Just over 70 percent of white law enforcement officers view these shootings as isolated incidents, but less than half of black law enforcement officers believe so. Even more telling, a majority of black officers (just like a majority of the public) view these shootings as indicative of a deeper problem within law enforcement regarding the black community.

At the same time, over 80 percent of officers say their department does not have enough manpower, while only 57 percent of the public feels that way.

Perhaps even more striking is the difference in how police and the general public view risks and frustrations of law enforcement officers. While 83 percent of Americans say they "understand the risks and challenges" faced by police, 86 percent of law enforcement officers say the public "does not fully comprehend the trials that officers face."

The study found that 83 percent of the public believe that officers "fire their service weapon" at least once in their career, when in fact only about 27 percent of officers actually do. The PEW study suggests some of this disconnect can be attributed to "vividly choreographed shootouts."

Interestingly, while 42 percent of officers have serious concerns about their safety, only 14 percent of the general public fear for their own safety. At the same time, 51 percent of officers and only 29 percent of all working Americans say they are "frustrated or somewhat less fulfilled" in their jobs.

In reviewing these numbers, we have to ask: Why such disconnect between the perceptions of white officers and black officers? Why such a disconnect between the perspectives of officers and the general public? These are important questions to ask. And we will attempt to answer some of those questions throughout this book.

## Professional Bias

While much of the public may not actually know or understand "professional bias," they often feel it during interactions with law enforcement. We'll review a stinging online article from *Topten.com* entitled "Top ten biggest reasons people hate police." The article suggests "10" reasons, but the author actually listed "50" reasons. And while much of the article was intended as sarcasm, the author did make some relevant points. Below are just a few of them.

I would offer that it is particularly important for individual law enforcement officers to review this list and try to discern what actions they may or may not be doing to cause members of the public to think such critical things about their profession.

If nothing else, the list clearly suggests that it is the actions of individual officers – not the actions of entire departments – that can often cause such negative sentiment among the public. I think the list also highlights why "community policing" alone isn't the answer to all law enforcement ills.

- **They are working for the politicians and not for the people.** The author suggests that police do not at all "serve and protect" the people, but rather serve only to "watch" the people and do not at all believe in "innocent until proven guilty."
- **They think they can talk and treat you however they want.**

As the author wrote, "Police officers are, for the most part, people of average to slightly below average intelligence. They tend to be sociopolitically conservative, narrow minded bullies who exhibit passion and prejudice on a daily basis. When I go outside, I'm not worried about the criminals. No criminal ever gave me a ticket or bullied me. I'm worried about the cops!... Just about all of them that I have ever met have a chip on their shoulder too."

- **They're stupid.**
- **They're criminals in disguise.** The author cites instances when police falsify and/or exaggerate reports.
- **They hate black people.** The author is suggesting that as the criminal justice system has been corrupt and immoral, and police officers wholly supported that corrupt, immoral criminal justice system, that makes police officers corrupt and immoral.
- **They think they own you.** The author offers instances of police officers simply disrespecting the public in everyday conversations.
- **They arrive on the crime scene after the story is over.** Great point here, as the author is recognizing current law enforcement's reliance on "response," rather prevention.
- **They're mean.** Far too many citizens have not had "positive" interactions with law enforcement. This should take us back to my suggestion that cops need to learn to initiate "smiles."
- **They abuse their power.**
- **They harass innocent people.**
- **They profile you based on what you look like.** This is actually a good point, but the truth is, profiling is simply good police work. Although, it certainly can be abused.
- **They do not respond to calls, especially during might time.**
- **They ask you questions that's none of their business.** Good point, but we know that officers often ask seemingly unimportant questions to "gauge" your response. Yes, they are trying to gather information. Unfortunately, this is antagonizing when one hasn't done anything. Therefore, this is indeed a reason many people disrespect police officers.

## Confirmation Bias

> *"If everybody is thinking the same thing, then someone isn't thinking."*
> *- George Patton -*

Think for a moment about the differences in everyday discussions between, say, a group of loggers compared to the topics of discussion among construction workers. They would probably have different things to talk about, right? Of course, they would. They have different objectives in their jobs, different safety precautions to follow, and even use different tools.

We can say the same about doctors versus teachers, lawyers versus restaurant managers, and any number of differences between untold numbers of professions. We can easily recognize why members from each respective group seem to understand each other better, or have the same or similar ideas, and often don't really understand the "how to" of other professions.

This is because they each speak a different language (of sorts), specific to their respective professions. Even the differences in occupations can create significant biases among groups of professionals. We should take just a moment to review how significantly these biases can affect our judgement, and how that may apply to the law enforcement profession.

In my 2008 book, *The Psychology of Management*, I explained a very important bias which should be considered in any discussion of group behavior. It is what the psychological community calls "confirmation bias." It can be defined as the tendency to overly rely on information that "confirms" what you – or your group – already thinks.

We call that information "confirming information." Of course, confirming information would be the exact opposite of "dis-conforming information," which is information that "disconfirms" what we already believe.

Confirmation bias can be a major obstacle in much of our decision making because, as human beings, we can reduce our most basic psychological needs down to two very simple things. Those two things are (1) we have a need to be liked and (2) we have a need to be right.

We like confirming information because it proves we are right. We like confirming information so much that we will go out of our way to find it and believe it's true, even if there is clear evidence that that confirming information is entirely false.

Of course, this is not always the case with all people. Higher education and/or experience can often (but not always) help us learn not to rely too heavily on confirming information. At the same time though, higher education and/or experience can also sometimes actually cause us to rely too much on confirmation bias.

Experienced professionals might find themselves succumbing to confirmation bias when they fall into the trap of "the way we do things around here." If you've ever heard someone tell a new employee that "this is the way we do things around here," you can almost be sure that person is very susceptible to confirmation bias.

A much better way to succeed in your work, in research, in decision making, etc. is to always look for – and even eagerly seek – disconfirming information, or to re-emphasize, information that disproves what you already think. The person who does this will make it much easier to avoid making errors in their reasoning.

It is because of the scourge of confirmation bias that George S. Patton is quoted as having said, "If everybody is thinking the same thing, then someone isn't thinking."

One of the most important things to remember about confirmation bias is that it can be very prevalent in high-performing teams or in groups with a good sense of camaraderie (like in the law enforcement profession).

Research on confirmation bias suggests that people – or groups – not only tend to accept information that they enjoy, or which fits their own personal or group narrative, they will actually focus only on that information, and ignore – and even fight against – other information or ideas. This can be particularly damaging when the information being ignored happens to be accurate, relevant and factual.

To reiterate, we tend to succumb to confirmation bias because we are afraid of being wrong.

As we can certainly classify the law enforcement profession as possessing a high degree of camaraderie among its members, it makes them very susceptible to confirmation bias. Our concern is that the forces involved in confirmation bias can cause the law enforcement community to suffer a form of *Déformation professionnelle*, meaning the tendency to see things strictly through the lens of one's own profession,

Again, this causes one's profession to ignore the thoughts, ideas and perspectives of other professions, or groups. If you've ever heard a law enforcement representative give the ever-recurring "Yall don't know what it's like" speech, you're likely to concur that my argument might actually hold water.

I believe several themes in this book will point to areas where law enforcement has fallen for this very easily avoidable cognitive bias. It is my hope the profession might recognize some of those instances and take advantage of opportunities to correct any *faux pas* which may have helped to contribute to the bad image of the profession.

These psychological concepts are not difficult to understand. In fact, they seem quite simple. So, it should be equally simple to consider that law enforcement officers are very likely to view every encounter only through the lens of "detention, arrest and documentation," as these are a very important aspect of their profession.

If we accept the very simple explanation of *Déformation professionnelle*, we can see how many interactions between law enforcement and the public can – intentionally or not – create friction, when a much better interaction with the general public should involve collaboration.

Any undergrad psychology student will tell you that professional bias can force us to place people in "silos" where we create an "us versus them" environment in which each profession speaks its own unique language, impeding their working with other professions. This "silo effect" is much of what has happened in the last few years between law enforcement and the public.

And to be clear, I'm suggesting that because of this deformity of thinking (which is what it is), law enforcement has created an organizational culture that has greatly separated its officers from the general public. If this is true, if it has any merit, then what could be some of the causes of such a restrictive professional bias within the law enforcement community? An important place to start would be law enforcement training.

## Where's the training for empathy?

We can gather initial insight into law enforcement training from a July 2016 report by the U.S. Department of Justice, Office of Justice Programs, Bureau of Justice Statistics (BJS). Entitled "State and local law enforcement training academies, 2013," it was conducted by Brian A. Reeves, a BJS statistician.

It found that between 2011 and 2013, an average of almost 45,000 police academy recruits entered U.S. police training programs each year. About one in seven were female, and about 1/3 were minorities.

An initial breakdown of areas of study and average number of hours for each area of study included;

- *Operations (213 hours)*
- *Firearms, Self-defense and Use of Force (168 hours)*
- *Self-improvement (89 hours)*
- *Legal Education (86 hours)*
- *Community Policing (over 40 hours)*
- *Domestics violence (13 hours)*
- *Mental illness (10 hours)*

In this list, we see that the majority of training that police recruits receive is in the area of "Operations." This includes patrol procedures (52 hours), investigations (42 hours), emergency vehicle operations (38 hours) and report writing (25 hours).

The second highest number of hours in training was spent on Firearms (71 hours), Self-defense (60 hours) and Use of Force (21 hours). Within the Use of Force category were included agency policies, de-escalation tactics and crisis intervention. In addition, the majority of recruits also received training in weapons retention, verbal command presence, pressure-point control and speed cuffing.

It is actually no surprise to find that police recruits receive a lot of hours in firearms training. Obviously, we don't want officers walking around who don't know how to handle a firearm professionally.

However, we should see warning signs when we notice that a combined 130 hours of training is spent on Firearms and Self-defense, while only 21 hours is given for Use of Force (which could include very important de-escalation and crisis intervention techniques).

This is very important to consider when we ask what kind of organizational culture the law enforcement community is creating. What message are young recruits receiving — and carrying into their new careers – when training on a weapon you'll probably never use in the line of duty is given much, much more focus and priority than de-escalation and crisis intervention skills, which officers - particularly patrol officers, if we believe the "you don't know what it's like' narrative - may use dozens of times per week?

One inspiring new aspect of police training in recent years has been the concept of "reality-based" training, where officers receive more "realistic" training with the use of different scenarios for firearms, use of force continuum and even control tactics and self-defense. Between 70 percent and 90 percent of recruits receive training in these areas with the very important reality-based training.

Sadly, figures for the hours or percentages of reality-based training in de-escalation and crisis control are non-existent.

> "American police officers are among the best-trained in the world, but what they're trained to do is part of the problem."

The BJS study found that 97 percent of recruits received an average of over 40 hours in community policing, which included identifying community problems, the history of community-oriented policing, interacting with youth, using problem-solving models, environmental cases of crime and prioritizing crime and disorder problems.

Perhaps most damning, between 2006 and 2013, the average amount of recruit training on Firearms increased from 63 hours to 71 hours, while hours in criminal and constitutional law decreased from 64 hours to 53 hours. The hours of instruction on patrol procedures decreased from 58 hours to 52 hours.

In December 2014, Seth Stoughton – former police officer, then professor of law at the University of South Carolina – penned a prolific piece about what he views as the inadequacies of police training. Entitled "How police training contributes to avoidable deaths: To save lives, cops must be taught to think beyond the gun belt," it insists that police shootings are much less about "racist cops" than about cops simply doing what they have been trained to do. As Stoughton wrote, "American police officers are among the best-trained in the world, but what they're trained to do is part of the problem."

He tells of graphic police academy videos shown to the newest recruits ingraining in their first few weeks that "complacency kills." From leaning too far into a vehicle and being shot, to warnings that a culprit can come at you with a knife from 20 feet away before you can draw your service weapon, all of which meant to implant that "vigilance" is of the utmost important and that "hesitation can be fatal."

Stoughton's most glaring revelation is that;

> *"In most police shootings, officers don't shoot out of anger or frustration or hatred. They shoot because they are afraid. And they are afraid because they are constantly barraged with the message that that they should be afraid, that their survival depends on it. Not only do officers hear it in formal training, they also hear it informally from supervisors and older officers. They talk about it with their peers. They see it on police forums and law enforcement publications."*

Again, his suggestion is that officers be taught that their guns, tasers and batons are truly weapons of last resort and that more emphasis should be placed on training officers to "think beyond the gun belt."

## Stressful Jobs

Perhaps one of the most eye-opening things I read in researching for this book came from a brief article entitled "9 most stressful American jobs in 2018," highlighting Kyle Kensing, the online content editor for *CareerCast.com*. When asked why some people may choose stressful types of work, he said very simply, "it's about the impact they can have."

Some folks are just adrenaline junkies. They crave risk. Also, while jobs that involved working closely with the public are considered some of the higher stress-related jobs, some folks are good at working with others, and some people just aren't. When it comes to police work, a lot of one's daily routine is going to include interacting with the public.

While I am sure the majority of people who choose law enforcement work do so because they know they'll work closely with the public, and they look forward to "making a difference," the law enforcement community needs to do better at identifying those who are simply not fit for working closely with the public.

While we're on the topic of stressful jobs though, it is interesting to consider that some of the "least" stressful jobs in the United States are;

- Jeweler
- Hair stylist
- Audiologist
- Medical records technician

As for *CareerCast's* actual nine most stressful jobs, they are listed below, from most to least stressful (with their corresponding salaries);

1. Enlisted military personnel - $26,054
2. Firefighter - $48,030
3. Airline pilot - $105,2704
4. Police officer - $61,6005
5. Event coordinator - $47,350
6. Reporter - $37,8207
7. Broadcaster: $56,680
8. Public relations executive $107,320
9. Senior corporate executive: $181,210

At least for a moment, let's stay on the topic of "stressful jobs," but let's throw in some unexpected perspectives that might be a bit embarrassing. A 2015 piece by *Payscale.com* entitled, "4 scientific reasons why waiting tables is the most stressful job out there," gives us some almost hilarious insight.

Let's be honest and admit that a recurring complaint from law enforcement officers is that they have to deal with "the public" every day. Seriously, we hear cops say that all the time. But let's also acknowledge that people who work in "food service" jobs — waiting tables, in particular — also deal directly with the public every day, all day.

According to *Payscale.com*, researchers at the Southern Methodist University in Guangzhou, China found that waiting tables is "the most stressful job" for many reasons. First, the pay is not great, averaging only about $24,325 per year, and very often includes "shift work." Additionally, they not only get complained to for things that are out of their control, the job is physically demanding.

All of these factors create the precise cocktail for work-related stress, leading to depression, and a host of other psychological factors, to include even alcoholism and drug abuse.

Of course, law enforcement comes with many hazards not experienced by wait staff. The point though is that law enforcement officers should keep in mind that "wait staff" - and other types of workers with very stressful jobs - hear officers complain about the stresses of "dealing with the public" and they aren't very sympathetic.

Cops should understand that — for the most part — the general public certainly understands the hazards that can come with serving in law enforcement. That's very likely why so many are unwilling to serve in law enforcement themselves.

Still, pick up any law enforcement magazine and it will surely have an article — if not several articles — about the "stress" related to law enforcement work. It's like the law enforcement community is infatuated with it, and – as we'll explore further in coming chapters, it's a telling sing of the "psyche" of the profession.

The sad truth is, when the public hears law enforcement complain about "stress" at work, those complaints fall the same on our ears as do the complaints of McDonald's workers demanding $15 per hour.

Yes! All jobs have their own elements of stress; some more than others. And, Yes! The stressors that come with being a cop are unique. We would tell a waiter that if he can't handle waiting tables at a restaurant – which can be fast-paced and very stressful – that he should probably seek a different type of work.

By the same token, if being a cop is too stressful for you, maybe you're just not cut out to be a cop. Why is that so taboo to say? We need to apply the same disciplined responses to law enforcement that we apply to another types of employment.

Law enforcement officers – and indeed all first responders – can and should take comfort in knowing that today's advanced training is designed specifically to help reduce work-related stress and is designed to do so specifically in their profession. Borrowed in large part from both military training and sports medicine, most law enforcement officers - and certainly many in the general public - have no idea how advanced training has actually become.

While we may "think" we would act certain ways in certain situations, under extreme stress we are in a very real sense "programmed" to act certain ways, without even thinking about it. Fortunately, we've finally learned that we can actually train our bodies – and more importantly, our minds – to overcome what evolution has implanted in us. And this new training to "re-program" our thinking has happened in just the last two decades or so.

In the last few years we've heard terms like "realistic training," but many of us don't really know the extent of how realistic our training is designed. These advances include using computer-generated "shoot-don't-shoot" scenarios rather than "paper targets" to the introduction of Simulated Rounds that actually "hit" trainees — often with some degree of pain involved — to program trainees to keep fighting even after they're "hit."

Other advances include introducing officers to the idea that during instances of extreme stress they might experience things like tunnel vision, seeing things in "slow notion," loss of memory or "mis-remembering" events. The advancement of course is that if officers "know" these reactions are normal, they know to expect them, and perhaps more importantly, not to be psychologically affected by them when they happen.

As a result of these types of advancements in our training, psychological reactions like PTSD are not what some have made them out to be. However uncomfortable it may be, we will discuss this much further in our chapter *PTSD and Law Enforcement*.

Unfortunately, bad things can happen during police encounters. A cop can make a mistake; say, an arrest that involved an inappropriate level of use of force, or maybe even a bad shooting. The first thing we do is blame the cop for his or her actions, and departments change polices to satisfy knee-jerk politicians, and even the media.

What we often miss is that we should be looking at that officer's training. We should be asking what training did he or she receive, or not receive? Why did the training not work? What training is out there that we didn't know about that could prevent this from happening in our department again? Instead, we often see administrators change department policy, many times resulting in further restricting what cops can and can't do — which only puts their safety in further jeopardy.

## Police personality

I mentioned earlier that the law enforcement community seems to be infatuated with the concept of job stress. We will examine that further in coming chapters, but a good place to start is to look further into already existing research on what is called "police personality."

From a psychological perspective, the current debate over police personality seems to be over whether it is a predisposition in one's personality (which drives the person into law enforcement) or is the personality a product of socialization within the law enforcement community (which forces officers to 'adopt' the personality simply to exist in the profession).

If the latter, the law enforcement community needs to do better not to create a culture that separates its officers from the people they serve. If the former, is a person with police personality – by definition – more susceptible to stress-related depression, PTSD, etc?

I believe that anyone genuinely concerned for officer safety would agree that these are legitimate and important questions to ask.

The "Behind the Badge" survey found that an alarming 56 percent officers say they have become "more callous toward people since taking their job." This should send a message of sincere concern as the survey also found that;

> "Officers who report they have grown more callous are also more likely than their colleagues to endorse aggressive or physically harsh tactics with some people or in some parts of the community. They are also more likely than other officers to say they are frequently angered or frustrated by their jobs or to have been involved in a physical or verbal confrontation with a citizen in the last month..."

In fairness, we should take into consideration that officers who are "involved in a physical or verbal confrontation with a citizen" are very much more likely to be patrol officers who have much more exposure to the public, often under adverse conditions. So, it would seem to reason that they might be "angered or frustrated," but that 56 percent said they were is still troubling.

At any rate, don't lose focus on the concept of "police personality," because we're going to examine it in depth in coming chapters.

# CIVILIAN PSYCHOLOGY

*"Be kind, for everyone you meet is fighting a hard battle"*
*– Plato –*

## Police recruitment

American writer and intellectual Gore Vidal is credited with saying, "We must always remember that the police are recruited from the criminal class." This is not far removed from the words of Lt. Col. Dave Grossman – author of the book *On Combat*, and a favorite trainer of the military and law enforcement – who very often says "there is a little bit of wolf in every sheepdog."

If the words of Vidal and Grossman are incorrect, then where are law enforcement officers recruited from? This year's graduates from Harvard Law School? The most recent graduating class of the United States Military Academy at West Point? While some of those elite graduates may go on to serve with federal agencies like the FBI or Secret Service, you will not find them filling out job applications for your local police department.

Though many law enforcement officers may later choose to advance their schooling with a bachelor's degree, you will not even find droves of graduates from your local college bachelor's degree program joining the rank and file of your local police department. And there's a reason why. And it's not just because of the fallacy of low pay.

Focusing specifically on IQ levels, we find a 2015 report by *PressTV* quoting controversial statements by former CIA contractor Steven Kelley who said that police departments across the country routinely do not hire applicants with higher level IQs.

In 2017, former law enforcement officer Mike McDaniel penned a piece entitled "Police IQ Trends" (It was actually an updated version of his 2014 "Police IQ" article). Intending to show that what he wrote in 2014 was getting even worse, he wrote that law enforcement agencies typically hired candidates who were "only smart enough, but no smarter."

While an average IQ between 85 and 115 is shared by about 68 percent of people in the country, a 2011 report by *CareerCast.com* showed the following law enforcement IQ levels;

> *Corrections officer - 96.6*
> *Police officer - 100.9*
> *Highway patrol officer - 102.3*

A November 2016 piece in *PoliceOne* online magazine entitled "Police loosen standards for accepting recruits" didn't help police image either. It revealed that not only were education standards for police candidates being lowered nationwide, acceptance of past drug use was being accepted as well.

Surprising to some, the issue of intelligence and law enforcement officers actually goes back as far as 2000, when Robert Jordan – a 39-year old college graduate – took his local police department's intelligence test in New London, Connecticut. Jordan scored a 39 (meaning he had an IQ of 124). Unfortunately, the department only interviewed candidates who scored between 20 and 27.

Jordan sued the city alleging discrimination, but the court ruled that he was not discriminated against because the police department applied the same standard to all applicants.

## An Objective Look at Officer Deaths

To put law enforcement officer line-of-duty deaths into at least some kind of perspective, let's use some very well documented history to do some very basic math.

World WWII ended in 1945 with the surrender of Germany on May 7th, then Japan on August 15th. As a result of this global war, about 400,000 Americans were killed. U.S. Census Bureau records estimate the population of the United States at that time to be just short of 140,000,000 (140 million).

For the U.S. Civil War – which ended in 1865 – estimates of the number of casualties vary, but most average about 720,000 killed. The U.S. population when the war ended was about 35,000,000 (35 million).

As a review, here are round numbers of American deaths during the following wars;

*Vietnam War deaths by year*
*1965 - 1,863 killed (5 per day)*
*1966 - 6,143 killed (17 per day)*
*1967 - 11,153 killed (31 per day)*
*1968 - 16,592 killed (45 per day)*
*1969 - 11,616 killed (32 per day)*
*1970 - 6,081 killed (17 per day)*
*1971 - 2,357 killed (7 per day)*

**Total World War II deaths by 1945** = 400,000
**U.S. Population in 1945** = 140,000,000

**Total U.S. Civil War deaths by 1865** = 720,000
**U.S. population in 1865** = 35,000,000

The numbers above show that the United States lost an average of 182 people every day during the four years of World War II, and an average of 513 people every day during the six years of the U.S. Civil War. Compare these numbers to the number of officer deaths each year listed by the Officer Down Memorial Page (ODMP) online, listed below;

*2010 - 181*
*2011 - 187*
*2012 - 142*
*2013 - 132*
*2014 - 159*
*2015 - 165*
*2026 - 174*
*2017 - 174*
*2018 - 163*

To be absolutely clear, any loss of a law enforcement officer is tragic. These deaths can be devastating to the officer's family and to his or her department and community of service. The loss of an officer can even be felt by officers in neighboring departments who may have occasionally worked or trained with that officer. Although, it should be important to put these officer deaths into some sort of perspective. Using the numbers of other professions might allow us to do so.

In January 2019, *USA Today* published it's "25 most dangerous jobs in the US" list. As we speak about the dangers of being a law enforcement officer, the list is particularly relevant – if not downright surprising.

## CIVILIAN PSYCHOLOGY

Below, the 25 jobs are listed from 1 to 25, in descending order (from most dangerous to least dangerous).

Along with the title of each job, we'll see the median income for that job. Keep in mind, this is not just 25 "random jobs," these are the 25 "most dangerous" jobs in America. The list is as follows;

1. Fishers and related fishing workers - $28,310
    Fatal injuries in 2017 - 100.0 per 100,000 workers
2. Logging workers - $38,840
    Fatal injuries in 2017 - 87.3 per 100,000 workers
3. Aircraft pilots and flight engineers - $111,930
    Fatal injuries in 2017 - 51.3 per 100,000 workers
4. Roofers - $38,970
    Fatal injuries in 2017 - 45.2 per 100,000 workers
5. Refuse and recyclable material collectors - $36,150
    Fatal injuries in 2017 - 34.9 per 100,000 workers
6. Structural iron and steel workers - $52,610
    Fatal injuries in 2017 - 33.3 per 100,000 workers
7. Driver/sales workers and truck drivers - $37,610
    Fatal injuries in 2017 - 26.9 per 100,000 workers
8. Farmers, ranchers and other agricultural workers - $69,620
    Fatal injuries in 2017 – 24.0 per 100,000 workers
9. First-line supervisors of landscaping, law service and grounds workers - $47,030
    Fatal injuries in 2017 - 21.0 per 100,000 workers
10. Electrical power-line installers and repairers - $69,380
    Fatal injuries in 2017 - 18.6 per 100,000 workers
11. Miscellaneous agricultural workers - $23,710
    Fatal injuries in 2017 - 17.7 per 10,000 workers
12. First-line supervisors of construction trades and extraction - $64,070
    Fatal injuries in 2017 - 17.4 per 100,000 workers
13. Helpers, construction trades - $30,120
    Fatal injuries in 2017 - 17.3 per 100,000 workers

14. *Maintenance and repair workers, general - $37,670*
    *Fatal injuries in 2017 - 16.6 per 100,000 workers*
15. *Grounds maintenance workers - $28,110*
    *Fatal injuries in 2017 - 15.9 per 100,000 workers*
16. *Construction laborers - $34,530*
    *Fatal injuries in 2017 - 14.3 per 100,000 workers*
17. *First-line supervisors of mechanics, $64,780*
    *Fatal injuries in 2017 - 13.1 per 100,000 workers*
18. *Police and Sheriff's patrol officers - $61,050*
    *Fatal injuries in 2017 - 12.9 per 100,000 workers*
19. *Operating engineers and other construction - $47,040*
    *Fatal injuries in 2017 - 11.8 per 100,000 workers*
20. *Mining machine operators - $53,200*
    *Fatal injuries in 2017 - 11.7 per 100,000 workers*
21. *Taxi drives and chauffeurs - $24,680*
    *Fatal injuries in 2017 - 10.5 per 100,000 workers*
22. *Athletes, coaches, umpires and related - $32,200*
    *Fatal injuries in 2017 - 9.5 per 100,000 workers*
23. *Painters, construction and maintenance - $37,960*
    *Fatal injuries in 2017 - 8.9 per 100,000 workers*
24. *Firefighters - $49,080*
    *Fatal injuries in 2017 - 8.9 per 100,000 workers*
25. *Electricians - $54,110*
    *Fatal injuries in 2017 - 8.4 per 100,000 workers*

The first thing we are likely to notice is that American military members do not appear on this list. This is because 2018 saw few military deaths due to drawdown of hostilities in Iraq, Syria and Afghanistan.

Next though, we see police and sheriff's deputies are listed at number 18. There is quite a difference in the numbers of deaths of law enforcement officers when compared to fishermen, loggers, roofers, garbage collectors, steel workers, farmers and electrical line installers. All had higher rates of death than law enforcement. Many of them with salaries far lower than that of law enforcement.

Have we bothered to ask ourselves why these American workers are not given similar services and widescale media attention as law enforcement officers?

Part of the answer is that law enforcement officer deaths in the line of duty most often involve another human being killing the officer. Indeed, this is what makes officer deaths so disturbing. Still, for family members, co-workers and the local community, the death of a logger when he or she is crushed by a fallen tree is also devastating.

The October 2018 funeral and services for Sgt. Terrence Carraway in South Carolina was reported by local news to have been attended by "more than 400 law enforcement officers from across the country."

As reported by the *Los Angeles Times*, at the Jan 25, 2019 services for fallen Newman Police Cpl. Ronil Singh, one could see "a sea of blue lined the pews" as it was attended by "hundreds of law enforcement officers from across the country." Also in January, as told of the services for Birmingham Sgt. Wytasha Carter, "Everywhere you looked you saw a badge from a different law enforcement agency… Officers from all over the country were here in Birmingham."

In May 2019, WLOX TV reported of the funeral of Biloxi Police Officer Robert McKeithen "a procession that included hundreds of law enforcement officers from across the country." Also in May, WTOC reported that at the funeral of Savannah Police Department Sgt. Kelvin Ansari, "multiple law enforcement agencies from across the country attended the service."

The services for Hall County Deputy Nicolas Blane Dixon – killed in the line of duty in July 2019 – was attended by "Hundreds of people, at least half in uniform."

Loggers, electricians, garbage collectors and any other number of American workers don't send their members to other states by the hundreds when a worker in their profession is killed on the job. So why does law enforcement do it?

Is it because the law enforcement profession is not as psychologically sound as other professions? Is it because the profession has created a psychological condition itself from demanding that the public feel exacerbated sympathy and compassion? When law enforcement officers receive that message over and over — in the media, in commercials, in their training, in glamorizing police funerals — are those officers predisposed to exhibit the signs and symptoms of a psychological response to trauma?

Again, this should not at all take away from the tragedy of the death of any law enforcement officer. It is simply a call to question why other much more deadly professions do not experience the anxiety that the law enforcement profession does.

At most of these funerals, we witness what is called "Last Call" or "End of Watch" ceremonies which, after an officer's death — usually in the line of duty — officers from his or her departmental listen on a department radio the "Last Call" to the officer, of which of course, he or she doesn't answer. The ceremony is to signify that that officer will no longer be responding to calls.

Indeed, societies throughout history have held special ceremonies specifically for their warriors. And many of these ceremonies were conducted by the warriors themselves. They have been absolutely important for the well-being of warrior societies, if not for individual warriors themselves.

Although, these "Last Call" ceremonies are now posted by the hundreds, if not thousands, on social media of individual officers, not as a result of their death, but on the day of their retirement. Even more intriguing, the videos are most often filmed by the retiring officer.

It's become predictable now that as the officer signs out on their department radio one last time, their faces are filled with tears. To go one further, departments have most recently even begun to have "Last Call" ceremonies for Canine officers.

This forces us to ask a very serious question: How did law enforcement get so soft and emotional? What happened to the tough image of the officer serving the community as a respectable, disciplined officer of the law? Say what you may, but at least acknowledge that this is yet another of the many things that some civilians often view as unusual about the law enforcement profession.

Again, other professions – many of which are more deadly than law enforcement – do not rally their members to drive hundreds of miles, across several states, to attend the funeral of someone they never met. Other professions do not post emotional "Last Call" videos of themselves to social media to show everyone how they cried at their retirement.

Psychologists say that the young female infatuation with taking recurring "Selfies" – and posting them on social media – represents an emotional response to how she views her body and how she wants to project her image to the world. Studies actually show that these young women often feel less confident and even less attractive after posting selfies.

Are the self-administered "Last Call" videos of law enforcement officers their own versions of how they want the world to view them? If so, why do they mimic what psychologist find to be most prominent among females, and less associated with masculine traits? Why do they want us to remember them in an uncontrolled, emotional breakdown?

It's a fair question!

## Say "Hello!"

According to the 2016 Cato Institute "Criminal Justice Survey," in the 1970s, 67 percent of whites and 43 percent of blacks had a "favorable" view of law enforcement officers. By 2016, the numbers were 68 percent and 40 percent, respectively. The numbers remained closely related, though black views showed a bit of a decrease. Still, other parts of the survey showed that no group (either white, blacks or Hispanics) was actually "anti-cop."

Interestingly though, only 62 percent of whites, 43 percent of African Americans and 49 percent of Hispanics rated their local police departments as "courteous." Those are not numbers that law enforcement should be proud of.

We might gain some insight into cop attitudes (as least as seen by the general public) from the 2017 "Behind the Badge" study. It found that while only 31 percent of law enforcement officers viewed their role as "protectors," a much lesser 16 percent of the public viewed them as protectors. In addition, while only 8 percent of officers viewed their role as enforcers, 29 percent of the public viewed them that way. I suggest those are troubling differences in opinions.

Lots has been written about how law enforcement officers appreciate when a member of the public tells them "thank you for your service," or buys them a cup of coffee, or a meal. Military veterans too know the feeling of appreciation that comes with such recognition.

Unfortunately for law enforcement, this doesn't happen as much as it should. However, far too many civilians are weary of even saying "Hello" to a law enforcement officer. Why? One reason is because so many civilians have simply had bad experiences with law enforcement; but we'll delve into that a little more later.

Another sad reason is that few civilians – as mentioned earlier – have ever had a law enforcement officer in uniform actually initiate a friendly "Hello!" on the street. Sure, an officer will return a greeting when one is offered, but the experiences of many civilians is that officers aren't naturally polite with strangers.

Of course, a rebuttal would be that law enforcement officers may not be as cordial as some would like, but it's because they must remain "vigilant." I think we've shown that that argument is a bit silly and does great damage to police-civilian relations.

> "How far that little candle throws its beams! So shines a good deed in a naughty world"

But, let's step back and take a deep breath here! Let's admit that it's a natural human tendency to question – if not overtly disdain – power and authority. And fewer people in history quantify that better than do Americans.

It's not shocking to suggest that law enforcement has given the public many reasons to question police actions and intent. Some people may well be justified in much of their distrust of law enforcement because they have actually suffered from abuse at the hands of an officer or a department in the past.

At the same time though, much of the anti-cop sentiment or distrust of police is simply our distrust and dislike of power and authority. Law enforcement would do well to remember this! For individual officers, it's not you they dislike, it's the position of authority.

All the more reason to put a smile on your face and just tell people "Hello" or "Good morning." I offer that in this very area is where law enforcement training has been its most neglectful. And it's revealed in the public's very well documented distrust.

One of the wisest characters in Shakespeare's many plays was that of the heiress Portia, in the play *The Merchant of Venice*. In that play, Portia says, "How far that little candle throws his beams! So shines a good dead in a naughty world."

Some may remember a version of that quote in the movie *Willy Wonka* when the candy maker told little Charlie, "So shines a good dead in a weary world."

The meaning behind the quote is that, even in a place of complete darkness, the smallest of candles gives off a bright light.

For civilians, I would offer that when you are disrespectful and dismissive of law enforcement, you are giving them the very power you say you disdain. Why argue with the police when all you're doing is placing an officer in a position where he or she has no choice – in the interest of their own safety – to interact with you with authority?

Lastly, the war on drugs has produced far too many occurrences where people are forced to interact with police when they otherwise would not have. Sadly, this very simple thing has been a major contributing factor to why people dislike law enforcement.

In a very real sense, citizens who feel they were unduly questioned, searched, arrested and jailed find injustice in their circumstance when they see the same law enforcement department allow looters to destroy property without repercussion, or watch rioters scream vulgarities in police officers' faces with impunity. While this may seem a bit petty, from a performance and motivation perspective, it makes a lot of sense.

Consider the grouchy waitress who complains about receiving poor tips from her customers. She contributes her poor work performance and unpleasant demeanor to stingy, non-tipping customers. In reality, she receives poor tips because she simply has a bad attitude and gives poor service.

We should not think that law enforcement is immune to the laws of performance and motivation. Cops with bad attitudes and distrust in the public breed distrust from the people.

# COMMUNITY POLICING

*"... to maintain at all times a relationship with the public that gives reality to the historic tradition that the police are the public and that the public are the police, the police being only members of the public who are paid to give full-time attention to duties which are incumbent on every citizen in the interests of community welfare and existence"*
*– Sir Robert Peel, known as "The father of modern policing" –*

## Broken Windows

The March 1982 issue of *The Atlantic* featured the claimed piece "Broken Windows" by George L. Kelling and James Q. Wilson, introducing what is called Broken Windows Theory. A very popular social gauge instrument for many social scientists and law enforcement, it is mostly unfamiliar to the public.

In short, Broken Windows Theory proposes that if a single broken window in a community is damaged – by a random baseball or even a vandal – but then repaired quickly, that sends a message to community members that ugly broken windows are not acceptable.

On the other hand, if a broken window is not repaired and allowed to remain broken, community members will begin to view ugly broken windows as acceptable. This is turn would encourage vandals to bust out more and more windows, and eventually encourage graffiti and other petty crimes.

The beat cop of former years was never far away when a neighborhood window was broken, and it wouldn't be long before he was able to inform the owner of the building of the eye sore.

In the same way an untreated minor infection of the body can lead to a major, life-threatening infection, according to Broken Windows Theory, ignoring petty crimes even encourages bigger crimes, causing the community to become more and more crime infested. In short, Broken Windows Theory suggests that – when it comes to preventing crime – the small things matter.

As we reviewed earlier though, foot patrolling actually restricts an officer and prevents him or her from responding to calls. There is also the argument that a Broken Windows approach focuses on smaller crimes, which inevitably targets minorities.

In researching for this book, one of the best opinions I came across was a March 2018 piece for Heritage Foundation, entitled "Cops count, Police matter: Preventing crime and disorder in the 21$^{st}$ century." Written by William Bratton – Senior Managing Director of Teneco and former NYC Police Commissioner – it superbly outlined where law enforcement exists today and the challenges it faces in the near future. For anyone in law enforcement, I would highly recommend reading it.

In it, Bratton lays out three important points that many are getting wrong about crime prevention. He insists that law enforcement can absolutely control crime and that precision policing is the way to do it. Secondly, while he acknowledges that bias does exist, he insists that any assertion that law enforcement is inherently racist is fundamentally wrong. While he acknowledges that some racial inequality may still exist, he believes that law enforcement is far ahead in addressing it than society at large

Lastly, while he believes law enforcement should continue its great efforts to resist bias, in order to control crime, law enforcement should focus on the "behavior" of criminals. His explanation acknowledges that certain small areas – and a handful of criminals – account for a majority of violent crimes. He insists that "targeted policing" to focus on that handful of individuals – rather than an entire community – should be the focus of law enforcement.

## What do cops think?

Pew Research shows that some 70 percent of law enforcement officers believe it is important that they understand the people in the neighborhoods they patrol. Interestingly though, the numbers vary across racial and gender lines.

As many as 84 percent of black officers and 78 percent of Hispanic officers say that understanding their patrol neighborhoods is "very important," while only 69 percent of white officers believe so. At the same time, 80 percent of female officers believe understanding is important, while only 71 percent of male officers do.

The overwhelming majority of white, black and Hispanic officers believe that relations between the police and white citizens is good. Those numbers are much different when dealing with other communities. Only 32 percent of black officers say that police relations in their neighborhoods are good, while 71 percent of Hispanic officers believe police relations in their neighborhoods are good.

Another important subset of opinions found that 56 percent of all officers believe that "in some neighborhoods being aggressive is more effective than being courteous." Pew also found that younger officers are more likely than older officers to believe aggressive methods are more effective.

Even more, 59 percent of rank-and-file officers – who are more likely to actively patrol the streets – are more likely to support aggressive methods, while only 34 percent of administrators believe so.

Lastly, 56 percent of officers say they have become "more callous toward people since taking their job."

An interesting side note here is to acknowledge that the overwhelming number of law officers never see the streets. That is to say, they never see the "real streets" – and many never will. Others will only see the streets for short periods of intermittent time. Very many officers are answering phones, booking and/or transferring suspects, filing or serving as guards. Still others are serving with special units like vice, strike forces, gang force units, etc.

For the most part, these officers do not respond to 911 calls. They are not patrolling in their communities, and they are certainly not interacting with the public as a "beat cop" would.

The purpose in the above introduction to this chapter is to show – in no uncertain terms – that law enforcement officers themselves differ widely not only in their opinions of their work and the methods used in their work, but also in the different kinds of work they actually do.

As we discuss community policing and the varying relationships between law enforcement and the public, this is important to consider. We can't paint all law enforcement officers with the same brush.

## Community Policing

Partly due to increased media attention on police use of force, and even implied racial tensions, American citizens have become more interested in how law enforcement conducts its training. In response, the *plan du jour* for law enforcement is to be more proactive in creating positive interactions with the media, the public, mental health agencies, faith-based groups, and even other government and non-governmental agencies. Copied in part from other professions, law enforcement says it is "building partnerships" with other entities in their communities.

New positions of Public Affairs Officer (PAO) or Public Information Officer (PIO) have been created in all but the smallest departments to spearhead these "partnerships." The reality is that these positions have been created not only to help distribute important information during times of emergency, but to help law enforcement departments "get in front of" the media during tense police-citizen interactions.

Large private organizations implemented PAO and/or PIO positions decades ago to help protect company image and to protect investors. Law enforcement does the same thing to protect the image of the local county sheriff, or the local mayor in the case of city police. This is no secret. It's not big news. I have not at all just written some damning critique of law enforcement.

Law enforcement is just following the lead of the private sector which has had to deal transparently for much longer than has law enforcement. Why else do you think nearly every law enforcement department across the country has a Facebook account, a Twitter account, and any number of other social media accounts? Law enforcement uses the media – even social media – to "market" itself.

Unfortunately, the law enforcement profession historically has either done a terrible job at projecting a good image, or the media has been unfair to law enforcement. I think we can agree that it's been quite a bit of both.

When it comes to community policing efforts, some are quite ingenious;

> **High-Five Fridays** - *Officers stand in front of schools as students arrive so that kids get the opportunity to "high five" the officers on their way into school.*

> **Coffee with a Cop** - *Departments might partner with local restaurants to have officers reserve tables one morning so that community members or leaders can simply sit and have coffee with representatives of the local law enforcement agency.*

> **Walk and Talk** - *Officers are chosen to simply walk a neighborhood or shopping areas and are encouraged to talk to members of the public.*

> **Law and Your Community Program** - *An interactive program developed by the National Organization of Black Law Enforcement Executives (NOBLE) Officers to help teenagers age 13-18 better communicate and understand law enforcement.*

As an example of another intriguing effort, in November 2018, the mayor of Portland, Oregon announced he would be bringing a proposal to the city council for a pilot program to hire "non-sworn officers who do not carry guns."

Initial ideas included that the new officers would only respond to calls with a sworn officer but could also provide support by waiting on tow trucks at the scene of a car accident. Tentatively called Public Safety Specialists, or PS3s, the officers might also respond to "non-emergency calls" like "minor property crimes and nuisance calls."

While the "mounted patrol" officers in Portland – who serve on horseback – had previously been used as part of the police department's public relations (to soften the image of the police department), that program would be eliminated in order to fund the PS3 program.

A very nice Oct 2017 piece in The Global Citizen entitled "Media bias and law enforcement" explained what it called the recent "shift in the perception of police officers." It insists that police officers have become "the target of hate and scorn from the public they have been sworn to protect." And it blamed the media for it.

Specifically, it says the media has created hatred for cops with its "focus on negative interactions between law enforcement and the community and give little attention to the positive interactions."

As it further reads, "the media does nothing to back law enforcement, in fact they focus more intensely on the backlash against law enforcement and the violence against police." Even more to the point, and in a direct lashing of the media, it goes on;

> "In this socially conscious society we are in today, there is no aspect of a person or group that is acceptable to make generalizations about. We cannot make generalizations about a person or group based on race, religion, socioeconomic status, their profession, life choices, etc. However, there seems to be one exception which the media makes in this regard, that is law enforcement."

It is important that we juxtapose that concept with what we are told about community policing. Of the many aspects of community policing, all are geared to help give law enforcement a better image. However, the intriguing part is that, at every turn in community policing, law enforcement uses the media to help broadcast those efforts throughout the community.

This is precisely why High Five Fridays and Coffee with a Cop campaigns seem warm and cozy to some, but to many others, these are deceptions of the real relationship between the media and law enforcement. In a real sense, it makes law enforcement disingenuous.

## How law enforcement lies (as bad as do the media)

Heather MacDonald – a scholar at the Manhattan Institute – was featured in a 2016 PragerU video explaining actual statistics involving police shootings. She noted that in 2016, Harvard economics professor Ronald Fryer found "no racial differences" when studying officer-involved shootings.

She also referenced Lois James of Washington State University, who found that law enforcement officers are actually *more likely* to shoot an armed white or Hispanic suspect than an armed black suspect. Even more shocking was her citing a *Washington Post* study which found that of all persons who died by homicide, 12 percent of whites killed were killed by police and only 4 percent of blacks killed were killed by police.

She summarized that in major cities across the country, not only do blacks commit a grossly disproportionate amount of robberies, murders and assaults, of some 6,000 blacks killed each year, most of them are killed by other blacks; Not by whites and not by law enforcement.

As we learn more and more about these shocking numbers, Americans are coming to realize that it is not racism or police brutality that threatens blacks in America. The greatest thing that blacks in America have to fear today is other blacks.

Sadly, some have suggested that as departments continue efforts to appear less aggressive in black neighborhoods, and "community policing" continues to grow in popularity and requires more and more officers to implement its programs, we will – by definition – see reduced numbers of officers available to make a patrolling footprint in black neighborhoods. As a result, we can expect to see rising numbers of black homicides and other crimes. In many areas, we are already seeing it.

In the 2018 PragerU online video entitled "Cops are the good guys," former Milwaukee County Sheriff David Clarke said, "Today, police are more professional, better educated and better trained than at any time in their history."

We dare not argue Sheriff Clarke's point. A major problem though is the law enforcement profession simply sat on its bad public image for too long. The profession unwisely relied on the trust of the general public not to believe media and other organization's attempts to discredit it. They simply did little until it has almost become too late.

Law enforcement is now having to play "catch up" with costly community policing programs and videos of cops "gettin' down" and showing of their R&B "dance moves" in uniform at school football games and pep rallies in order try to "soften" their image. Many of these efforts though seem to create a weird sort of feminization of the profession, and it's simply making cops look silly and undisciplined.

That's not to say that law enforcement can't correct the negative image it has created for itself. It certainly can! But those efforts are going to have to include using policing data to show how inaccurate media images and portrayals have harmed not just cops, but the general public.

That will be a difficult hurdle though as it is often politically focused mayors, sheriffs and other elected officials who stand in the way. Many of them are the real enemies of today's officers.

# POLICE CANINES

*"If the only tool you have is a hammer, you tend to see every problem as a nail"*
*— Abraham Maslow —*

For law enforcement, searching for illegal drugs can be a difficult task, but departments across the country ensure us that using police canine "drug dogs" that can "sniff out" certain drugs have been a tremendous help in these searches while not intruding on individual rights.

Police canines are also used as "search dogs" to look for suspects who might be hiding from law enforcement. This too — we are told — has very likely saved uniformed officers from getting hurt, or even killed.

Although, others say that in efforts to help bridge the gap in relations between law enforcement and the public, departments today exploit the "man's best friend" variable, and that with police canines comes some heavy baggage.

While the use of police canines carries racial implications — stemming from videos of police using tear gas, firehoses and dogs against protesters during the Civil Rights era of the 1960's — which have unfortunately remained as one of the ugliest stains on police-civilian relations, there are much more recent and certainly more relevant cases in which the use of police canines have proven to be a tactic that is only serving to further damage law enforcement's image.

In 2003, the new commanding officer of the U.S. military prison at Guantanamo Bay (GTMO) Naval Base recommended the use of dogs during prisoner interrogations. Later, commanders at Abu Ghraib Prison in Iraq used dogs because of the success of their inducing fear among prisoners. There would later be reports from Abu Ghraib of U.S. service members using those dogs to abuse and humiliate prisoners.

Human beings have an inherent fear of many animals, especially if they fear those animals might attack them. The use of dogs at both GTMO and Abu Ghraib prisons was psychological, of course, intended to introduce an added variable to induce stress.

Maj. Gen. Geoffrey D. Mille – former team leader and commander at GTMO Bay – was quoted as saying that dogs were used at the prison because of "the Arab fear of dogs." Law enforcement knew that the same fear factor could be beneficial in their work back home in the United States.

Although, there is quite a lot to suggest that the use of dogs in law enforcement is not at all what it has been made out to be. In many ways, our inherent love for "man's best friend" is being exploited in inherently unethical ways.

## Show Heifers

Fewer things involved in law enforcement's interaction with the public are filled with more rhetoric – if not outright misleading information and lies – than that which has been generated about police canines.

For many in the public, there is a view that law enforcement has granted itself permission to search anyone at any time, for no particular reason, so long as there is an officer with a police canine available.

Perhaps surprising to some is the actual reliability of these animals. While the courts have held that a police canine "alerting" its handler of the presence of drugs constitutes "probable cause," significant research exists strongly suggests that these dogs are not as highly trained – or reliable – as they are purported to be.

The effectiveness of drug-sniffing dogs began to come into serious question as a result of a 2006 Australian study entitled, "Review of the Police Powers (Drug Detection Dogs) Act 2001," which focused on "general drug detection" in public places. The study found that drug-sniffing dogs had a success rate of only 26 percent. They failed three out of four times!

It further suggested that such high failure rates could be attributed to dogs not being able to distinguish between someone who may have been exposed to someone else's drug use and someone who actually had drugs in their possession. It also suggested that a drug-sniffing dog might "alert" on someone who may have smoked marijuana several hours or even days before the search. To think that such an "alert" constitutes probable cause is disturbing.

Even more, several studies suggest that most police canine searches result in law enforcement finding only small amounts of drugs intended for personal use rather than "trafficking." If true, there is serious question as to the cost-benefit of using these dogs.

Finally, the study noted that during drug-sniffing searches, "dogs can become tired, hungry, distracted by surrounding sights and noises." This too can cause dogs to "alert" (just to get it over with) or rely on its handler for "cues."

A later study in January 2011 by the *Chicago Tribune* analyzed the use of drug-sniffing dogs in Illinois. It too showed that these dogs were wrong more often than they were right. Analyzing several years of police data, it revealed that police canines were only right 44 percent of the time. Even more damning, the research showed that when a traffic stop involved Hispanic drivers, the dogs were only right 27 percent of the time.

In both studies, dog handlers and trainers argued that those numbers only show that dogs can often smell the "residue" of drugs that may no longer be there, meaning that there "were" drugs there, but the drugs are gone now. Although, the *Tribune* further reported that;

> "... even advocates for the use of drug-sniffing dogs agree with experts who say many dog-and-officer teams are poorly trained and prone to false alerts that lead to unjustified searches. Leading a dog around a car too many times or spending too long examining a vehicle, for example, can cause a dog to give a signal for drugs where there are none, experts said."

Yet another critical study on drug-sniffing dogs appeared in the May 2011 issue of *Animal Cognition* which focused specifically on "false cues" that dog handlers can give their dogs. The term "false cues" refers to how dog handlers (intentionally or not) can cause their dog to alert, even if the dog smells no drugs at all.

The study showed that when handlers believed there were drugs in a particular spot, they would "cue" their dogs to "alert" on the spot, in an attempt to prove their dog was performing correctly.

Though some dog handlers questioned the research methods of this study, it was a particularly shocking one for the dog handler community as it raised the fear that dog handlers could actually "cue" their dogs during a real-world roadside traffic stop, leaving open the opportunity for police to justify in court what could clearly be an improper, if not illegal, search.

Even before researching the issue for this book, I was always intrigued by the use of police canines in drug searches. Having grown up rodeoing and being around very well-trained roping horses, I know what a well-trained animal looks like and how it performs.

In watching these dogs, it always seemed clear to me that they seemed either confused or more focused on their handlers than on the job at hand. It was clear to me that the dogs were trying to figure out what the handlers wanted them to do.

I always put those thoughts aside, convincing myself that I was not an expert on the way police canines are trained, so it was unfair for me to critique how they "alert." After reviewing the current literature and research on police canines though, I realized that my initial instincts were not wholly inaccurate.

As a result of the above and other studies, "handler bias" has clearly become a concern. If dog handlers themselves are aware of handler bias, and they still support the use of police canines, this may itself call into serious question the integrity of those handlers themselves. That is yet another reason why many might question the integrity of all law enforcement.

Of course, the point here is that departments who use police canines would do well to better address these concerns with the public. And if the accuracy of police canines really does hover around 50/50, their credibility is in serious question. But, there's more bad news about these dogs.

## Dogs Gone Wild

As part of "community policing" programs across the country, many departments exhibit their police canines at local festivals and even school functions. The exhibitions are intended to garner support for the department using "man's best friend." Who doesn't love a dog, right?

Cell phone videos and even body cams may show instances when law enforcement officers may be out of control, but footage of the excessive force used of police canines is particularly disturbing. Also, while use of police canines is often very violent, many times innocent people are harmed.

While the law enforcement community may describe sterile terms like "detain" and "apprehend" when using police canines, the general public often sees a vicious animal gnawing a man's arm off.

Again, it's upsetting for some that the courts have given law enforcement such a wide berth in the use of dogs. As an example, the 2017 *Maney v. Garrison* case involved an excessive force case where a police dog mistakenly attacked the wrong person. It involved a gruesome attack that left an innocent homeless person with a laceration to the scalp and "deep puncture wounds" to his arm and thigh.

Though on a leash – under the supposed control of the dog handler – the dog attacked without command from the dog handler. The handler admitted that he knew the person being attacked was not the suspect being searched for and – once the dog attacked – the handler "made no attempt to command the dog to stop his attack."

The injured homeless man sued, "alleging a violation of his Fourth Amendment right to be free from unreasonable seizure." Ultimately, the 4th U.S. Circuit Court of Appeals ruled that police officers have no obligation to immediately stop a police dog attack, even if they know the person being attacked is not a suspect.

In October 2018, a U.S. district court judge ruled in favor of the Indianapolis Metropolitan Police Department (IMPD) in a case filed by a woman who was 7-months pregnant when an IMPD police canine attacked her instead of the suspect that police were actually pursuing. She would eventually undergo several surgeries because of the wounds to her arm and leg. Though the woman did nothing wrong, and was not at all a suspect, the judge ruled that the attack did not violate her constitutional rights.

In January 2006, 11-year-old Courtney McGarry was petting a police canine that law enforcement officers had brought to her school for a D.A.R.E program. The dog violently bit her face. The officer had previously told the students, "he won't bite." Local news reported that the dog remained on duty with the department because "the animal did what it was trained to do."

We could reference dozens upon dozens of these terrible dog attacks, but let's just focus on a few instances which occurred in the months leading up to the publication of this book.

In July 2018, the "prong collar" of a police dog in St. Paul, Minnesota unexpectedly broke. At that very moment, a 35-year-old man was leaving his home to go to work. The dog attacked the man. Despite the dog handler's efforts, the dog would not let go. Police ordered the innocent man to the ground, hollering at him to "Stop pulling sir! Stop pulling!" The dog attack resulted in the innocent man receiving a 4-inch laceration to his stomach, and puncture wounds to his arm.

A local St. Paul newspaper investigation found that "officers lost control of their K-9s on occasion, dogs regularly apprehended people with no instruction from handlers and that some bystanders were attacked while officers were following common practices." The mayor and police chief ultimately issued a joint statement wisely announcing they would restrict the use of police dogs in the city.

In September 2018, video was released of an August 2016 police dog attack in Roswell, Georgia. The dog attacked a 17-year-old black male who was obeying police commands. The gruesome video shows the dog latched onto the young man's arm, refusing to let go, even after his handler frantically pulled on its leash.

The dog finally released the man's arm then attacked again latching on to his hand. Again, the handler had to repeatedly pull on the dog's leash before it let go. The dog in fact ignored some 20 commands to let go. When the dog finally did let go the second time, it briefly attacked the handler. The dog was not taken out of service, but rather sent for "extra training."

Also in September, as a Columbus, Georgia police officer was training his police canine at the department training facility, the dog turned on him. The dog was so out of control that the officer had to shoot it to escape the attack. The officer received serious bites to both forearms requiring surgery.

Yet again in September, in Montgomery County, Maryland, several suspects crashed a car near where a lady was walking her dog. The suspects jumped out of the car and were chased by several officers and a police canine. The dog turned away from chasing the suspects and latched on to the innocent woman's leg, refusing to let go. The woman reported that it took several officers to get the dog to release its grip.

In October 2018, during a trick-or-trick event in New Castle, Indiana – while police officers were handing out candy – a police dog unexpectedly bit a child's left arm. In the same month, in Waco, Texas, while two police officers were serving a warrant, their police canine turned and attacked its handler. The officer was forced to shoot the dog.

In November, a Manatee County Sheriff's Department (MCSD) officer in Florida was dropping off his child at school. Unaware that a police canine was in the back seat, a schoolteacher opened the vehicle door to let the child out. The dog attacked the teacher, biting her in the stomach.

As the MCSD spokesman said, "It is part of the dog's training, when that rear door opens, they're ready to jump out, they don't go directly to attack mode, but they'll jump out and sometimes they'll run directly up to a person almost in a playful way, but people can be startled by that."

## Summation

Barry Cooper – one of the nation's most recognizable drug enforcement police officers – grew disappointed in the use of police canines. He now serves as an expert witness for the defense in cases involving police canines. Cooper says that police canines can be an asset for police departments, but hand and vocal gestures by a handler can cause a dog to "react." He says that – rather than focusing on the reliability of police canines – courts should focus on the reliability of dog handlers.

The website of the law offices of David Sloan in Fort Worth, Texas too supports the use of dogs in some areas of law enforcement activities, but insists that, "Those in which the officer claims the animal has been trained to sniff out illegal narcotics or marijuana pose the greatest threat to our Fourth Amendment protections against unreasonable searches and seizure by law enforcement."

As the law firm suggests, "False alerts routinely occur and this fact is concealed by law enforcement." The firm cites a 2007-2009 study by the Illinois Department of Transportation which found a search accuracy rate "as low as 32 percent with some agencies participating in the survey."

The point is, with police drug dog failure rates of up to some 75 percent, that means a lot of innocent people are being falsely accused of possessing illegal drugs and subjected to unreasonable searches. That has done much to damage the relationship between law enforcement and the people they are sworn to protect and serve.

In addition, we must also think critically about attacks by police canines. If a law enforcement officer were to beat a suspect who was on the ground, handcuffed, already detained and no longer a threat, wouldn't that officer deserve punishment? Yes! He or she would deserve punishment because it would be considered unreasonable force, if not outright cruel and unusual punishment.

Why is it somehow acceptable to seek punishment for someone who harms a police canine – as if that dog were an actual police officer – but excuse the canine when it attacks an innocent person because "that's what he's trained to do"?

Is it reasonable to suggest that a dog cannot be expected to understand when to "stop" in the heat of battle? To do so not only removes blame from the dog – and even the handler – we are somehow allowing blame to magically disappear.

In the case of a terrible police canine attack, if it's a mistake to blame the dog – since the dog is simply doing what it is trained to do – who then is at fault? One would think the trainer or handler, obviously. Then where are the trainers and/or handlers who have been prosecuted for unreasonable force?

A law enforcement officer can be called into question if he or she uses his or her debilitating spray, baton or sidearm. But if the dog is used, the officer is easily without blame.

We can find plenty of YouTube videos of police canines performing seemingly magnificent feats during routine demonstrations. We forget though that "demonstrations" are not the same as actual combat. When an animal gets into a fight – as we've seen in numerous videos of dogs subduing suspects – it is often very difficult to get that animal to disengage. And we have seen it time and time again.

Particularly disgusting is when we see video of a dog attacking a suspect, and a police representative says that the police dog continued to engage because the suspect refused to comply and was "resisting arrest." We must question if it is physically – or even mentally – possible for any human being to "stop resisting" when a 100-pound fierce animal – trained to inflict grotesque, overwhelming fear and panic and pain – is mauling your arm off.

Seriously! At least one time allow yourself to objectively watch a video of a dog attacking a human being in actual combat. Every single time the person is screaming bloody murder. For me, it's disheartening because while viewing these gruesome attacks, we very often hear some of both law enforcement and civilians say ridiculous things like, "don't do the crime if you can't do the time."

Doesn't this completely side-step our grand concepts of due process and 'innocent until proven guilty'? Just as cynical are those who even cheer and rejoice at the cruelty. It's disgusting and barbaric!

As an example of the absolutely nutty ideas some have about the use of police canines, below is a comment from a social media follower who answered one of my questions about the use of police canines. Unfortunately, many who support the use of these – often overly aggressive – these very aggressive animals feel the same as this guy;

> *"Law abiding persons like most of us, don't care how long the dog gets to enjoy his job. I worry more about the dog getting infected by the blood contamination from the criminal. If the criminal would have NOT run, NOT hide, NOT been disrespectful to law enforcement, then the dog would not have been brought out of the car. This country has the criminal element level it has, because criminals have too damn many rights and privileges. We hire and employ trained law enforcement to control the criminal element, but the legal system has become so damn biased against law enforcement, that Police are leaving the job, not putting as much effort into taking*

*down criminals, because there comes a point that by the time an officer determines whether he is in the right or wrong of a situation, the criminal has gotten away. Too many times Upper management, for PR reasons, throws the officer under the bus to save their own hides. K-9's are a necessary element in police work. Criminals are not going to be afraid of a dog with a Muzzle on them. You might as well quit using the K's and go to using a feline and tell the criminal you're going to throw this cat on them if they don't stop. The criminal needs to play dead, plain and simple."*

As San Diego Police Department canine handler Larry Adair said in one interview"

*"Our dogs bite... They bite and hold. It's trained behavior. We're looking to apprehend or stop a behavior and the bite and hold allows us to gain control of an individual, minimize the amount of damage that is done because by and large this bite is a couple of punctures and pressure as opposed to the multiple bites."*

Adair went on to explain how officers do not "remove" a dog by verbal command, but rather by physical force;

*"We remove the dog physically... Mechanical application of pressure on the dog's correction collar to forcibly remove them from the bite when it's safe to do so."*

Yes! You read that correctly! A police canine attack – even from a highly trained police dog – is so vicious and violent that police officers are unable to stop it. They have to induce severe pain on the dog to get him to release. And cosmetic words like "apprehend" and restrain" are used to hide the inability of canine handlers to control their animals. It's disgusting and barbaric!

Clearly contradicting what dog handlers tell us, a *Science Direct* study as early as 2006 found that police canine dog bite victims were typically bitten in the head, neck, chest and flank, and, also bitten multiple times. The devastation from police canine attacks was found to be much more violent than that of other canines as the victims of police canine attacks were hospitalized more often, and "underwent more operations and had more invasive diagnostic tests."

Said another way, police canine attacks are much more violent than attacks from other types of dogs.

In our age of ordinary citizens posting social media videos of police canines mangling our fellow citizens in the streets – and the public seeing the gory results of the attacks of these vicious animals – we are already seeing departments quietly backing away from their use. And that's a good thing!

Another reply to a social media post of mine regarding police canines speaks volumes. While these animals may certainly have a use in the most extreme of cases, they are not "fellow officers." They are animals! That law enforcement actually calls them "officers" is mindboggling and may well speak to the naivete of law enforcement thinking overall.

The responder's words were as follows;

> "I learned in Tactical Canine Medic Training that one of the most common people to shoot a police Canine is a LEO who got in the way. When a Canine is in attack mode it may be difficult to turn that Canine off. Canines are not accountable to human ethical conduct.... I mean this with both practicality and with empathy... dogs are both tools to be used and sacrificed in the police and military world and worthy of respect afforded in service. But we do not hold them as our equals."

# SOME REALLY WEIRD STUFF

> *"Policemen so cherish their status as keepers of the peace and protectors of the public that they have occasionally been known to beat to death those citizens or groups who question that status"*
> *— David Mamet, American playwright, film director, screenwriter and author —*

### Resisting Arrest

Some have suggested that the growing numbers of "resisting arrest" charges are actually due to officers using the charges in order to "cover up" police brutality. And there may be some truth to those accusations.

A recent five-year analysis of the New York Police Department found that of nearly 50,000 resisting arrest charges, 75 percent of the charges were filed by only 15 percent of the department's officers, and half of the charges were filed by only 5 percent of the department's officers. The study also discovered that a single officer had been responsible for 10 lawsuits within just two years.

While this may paint a very ugly picture for all of law enforcement, it does give credit to the idea that there are bad apples everywhere. Even while this very damning NYPD study may show that resisting arrest charges had been rising, it also shows that most NYPD officers are not responsible for those charges.

Still, as lawsuits can cost cities and counties millions of dollars – and since law enforcement departments like to spend untold dollars on the latest technologies – much of the public wonders why departments don't spend more time and effort weeding out bad officers, which could save communities untold numbers of dollars. Especially when – according to the NYPD analysis –as many as 15 percent of officers are abusing their authority. That's a bit more than just "a few bad apples.",

With almost any social media video of police having to deal with a person who is actually resisting arrest comes exuberant outbursts from people who think the officers were too aggressive. Perhaps the worse though are those who laugh saying things like, "It took five cops just to take down that one guy."

On one hand, few instances give folks a better reason to charge cops with aggressive behavior than when cops are trying to subdue a non-compliant person. Still, for some people, it's not simply that the suspect might have been so badass that it took five cops to bring him down, the perspective is actually one borne out of a desire to want cops to look weak. So, let's put this nonsense to rest right here and now!

We can have no doubt that there are people reading this book who have never really been in an actual fight. I don't mean a shoving match, or a really intense exchange of vulgarities, I mean a knock-down-drag-out in a barroom parking lot where some guy is literally trying to beat the living shit out of you.

There are those of you reading this book though who have been in that kind of fight. Those people know full well – because they've been there – that it doesn't matter what size someone is or what training they might have had, you know that the certainty of who is going to win the fight won't really be known until the fight is over.

Why? Because you might slip on a damn rock. You might accidentally fall and seriously hurt your wrist. That guy you were sure you could beat could suddenly pick up pool cue stick, totally changing the odds of the fight. Or, he could pull out of knife, which means you just chose to fight a guy who is willing to go to jail for murder.

The point of course, is that when two or more human beings get into a fight, there are so many possible scenarios that there is absolutely no way to know exactly how the fight is going to end until it does actually end.

But, when it comes to law enforcement officers, we have one other very important variable that is probably the most important of all. Departmental policies!

Very often when a suspect does not want to be detained or handcuffed, he or she will do everything in their power to get away from law enforcement. That includes the opportunity to run, fight, kick, punch, throw things, try to find a weapon, attempt to grab an officer's weapon, or pull their own weapon.

For the officers, they are required to use only that which they absolutely need to get the suspect subdued. That means you can't just pull their sidearm and shoot if a guy spits in your face. You can't use your sidearm to crack the guy over the head. You can't use your baton to intentionally hit the guy in the head, in the spine or in the groin. Why? Because all of those choices are considered excessive use of force.

When a person makes the decision to resist arrest, the result is going to be an escalation of the conflict. For the officer, or officers, present, everything they do should be focused on de-escalation. That means they should (and must) use only the level of force necessary to enact what they are actually trying to do, and no more.

So, if five officers are forced to have to take down a guy, a tussle will obviously begin, but – once they can get the guy on the ground – one officer can contain one leg, another officer can contain the other leg. The same with the arms, until the person is completely under control, so they can be handcuffed.

If an officer has to handcuff the same guy alone, that one officer will be forced to use much more aggression that each of the five officers would have. The point is, having five officers subdue a guy is much safer for the officers and much safer for the subject!

Still, fighting is a dangerous game, and even with five officers, there's a very good chance that at least a couple of officers are going to get hit, their uniforms are going to torn, and/or some of their equipment will break. The "It took five cops to take down that guy" are words spoken by idiots.

## Ferguson Effect

In August 2014, 18-year-old Michael Brown was shot and killed by a white officer in Ferguson, Missouri. It was yet another instance that sparked condemnation of police interactions – particularly those dealing with the black community – and widespread protests.

It produced the wholly inaccurate "Hands up, Don't Shoot!" cries across the country. As the objective among us know, the investigation into Michael Brown's killing found that not only was he not shot in the back, he didn't have his "hands up," and that he actually tried to grab officer Wilson's gun.

A January 2017 Louisiana State University survey entitled "Policing in post-Ferguson society survey" examined the post-Ferguson attitudes of law enforcement officers from across the country. In what should be the most shocking for citizens, the study found that 45 percent of officers said they were "less motivated" in their job and, 51 percent said they actually enjoyed their job less. While 95 percent of officers said they were confident in determining the proper use of force, 52 percent "were apprehensive about using it." Those are fascinating – if not frightening – numbers!

Even more, 43 percent of officers said they didn't feel safe on the job, and many were reluctant to "seek help," as even their own department-provided programs were suspect as officers feared "retaliatory actions" for seeking treatment. We will discuss this at length in our chapter *PTSD and Law Enforcement*.

While white and black officers disagree about police interactions within black communities, a staggering 80 percent of officers said that because of recent news coverage of deadly events, their already stressful and dangerous jobs are even more difficult now. And some 72 percent said they are "less willing now to stop and question people who seem suspicious or to use force when it is appropriate to do so." As an obvious correlation, 93 percent say they are more concerned for their safety.

According to the "Behind the Badge" study, a majority of officers (68%) say recent protests are the product of ongoing hatred of police. An equally large majority believe the events leading up to protests are actually isolated events, exaggerated by public outcry and unfair media attention.

Although, 57 percent of black officers say these deadly incidents are the product of real problems between law enforcement and the black community, while only 27 percent of white officers believe so. We have to ask what is the reason for such widely opposing opinions across racial lines within law enforcement?

Interestingly, police administrators are clearly more sympathetic to the motives of protesters, with 46 percent of them sympathetic to the idea that protesters simply want to hold police accountable, while only 34 percent of rank-and-file officers agree.

An early 2019 *Stanford Open Policing Project* report compiled data from over 100 million traffic stops from 21 different state patrol agencies conducted from 2011 to 2017. It found "pervasive inequality in how police decide to stop and search white and minority drivers."

NBC News covered the story quoting David Lowery – founder of the Living & Driving While Black Foundation in Chicago – who said, "There's no longer the idea of Officer Friendly, who might help you understand why they pulled you over. Now, it's about using racial profiling to control people and place fear in them."

Lowery was further quoted as saying, "Then, you've got money tied up in this… Who can write the most tickets? Who can put the most people in jail and into the court system? It's no longer about a simple traffic stop for safety."

Although, it should be understandable that law enforcement officers patrol high-crime areas more often than areas with low rates of crime. We should want our officers to patrol high-crime areas, so the bad guys see that the good guys are nearby.

As it is well established that very many high-crime neighborhoods have higher percentages of minorities, it should be further understandable that those minorities are more likely to come in contact with law enforcement (because there are more law enforcement officers present in their communities).

Other shocking numbers resulting from recent, fatal police-black encounters include the below. In what the "Behind the Badge" study calls "de-policing," the percentages of officers who answered affirmatively to these questions is alarming;

> *Increased fear for personal safety? 93%*
> *Reluctance to use force? 73%*
> *Increased tension between blacks and officers? 75%*
> *Increased reluctance to stop and question suspicious people? 72%*

A very unique perspective on police-citizen interactions – especially those involving black communities – can be gained from the 2017 Heritage Foundation report entitled, "Policing in America: Lessons from the past, opportunities for the future."

In it, Garry F. McCarthy – Police Director of the Newark Police Department from 2006 to 2011 and Superintendent of the Chicago Police Department from 2011 to 2015 – poignantly wrote, "Police do not engage in systemic racism by addressing crime patterns; what they are doing is intelligent policing." McCarthy says that misunderstanding this is the greatest danger facing law enforcement today.

Unfortunately, instances of police excessive use of force and brutality do occur. One very shocking contributor has become the use of "Tasers." When first introduced, Tasers were touted as a tool to allow officers to use "less lethal" force in dangerous situations. That is, a tool to help officers subdue a violent person without using lethal force. Shockingly though, as reported in a 2012 *Chicago Tribune* piece, Taser use by police "doubled" from 2008 and 2011.

Writing for *TheRoot.com*, Michael Harriot notes that law enforcement officers killed 1,129 people in 2017. In his bold piece entitled "I'm a black ex-cop, and this is the real truth about race and policing," Harriot notes that that's more than the number of American service members killed in action (21), more than the number of Americans killed by terrorists (four) and even more than the number of black people lynched in 1892, the worst year of the Jim Crow era (161).

Critics ask that if the use of Tasers was actually replacing the use of bullets, why have justifiable police shootings increased in the past decade rather than decreased? It's a serious question that we need to answer.

Writing for the *Washington Post*, Reddit Hudson – a former law enforcement officer – penned his own 2014 critique of law enforcement entitled "Being a cop showed me how racist and violent the police are. There's only one fix." Later serving as chair for the board of The Ethics Project, he wrote;

> "... more and more, I felt like I couldn't do the work I set out to do. I was participating in a profoundly corrupt criminal justice system. I could not, in good conscience, participate in a system that was so systematically unfair and racist. So after five years on the job, I quite."

Hudson added, "Unfortunately, I don't think better training alone will reduce police brutality. My fellow officers and I took plenty of classes on racial sensitivity and on limiting the use of force."

I think Hudson is right about racial sensitivity training. Most of it is not only garbage, it very often creates increased – not before present – tension and division, and even distrust. Although, I'm certain that he is wrong about overall training.

The public and the media may make ethical arguments about cops making mistakes, but many of us know better. In just the last two decades or so we've come to understand that many bad cop decisions are not due to bad or racist cops, they are due to the insufficient preparing of officers for better performance under stress.

In a November 20, 2018 piece, Kyle S. Reyes – spokesperson for *Law Enforcement Today* magazine – gives an interesting perspective derived from FBI statistics. In his piece entitled "FBI data proves cops are not racist killers" he found that with some 53,380,000 contacts that law enforcement officers make in a year, only about 26,000 resulted in a claim of "excessive force."

That's only 0.049 percent of all contacts. Even more, he found that of those 26,000 complaints, only 2,080 were sustained. That's a rate of only 0.0039 percent.

Focusing specifically on 2015 shootings, he found that of the 990 people shot by police that year, the racial classifications of those shot were;

> White - 494 (50%)
> Black - 258 (26%)
> Hispanic - 172 (17%)
> Other - 66 (7%)

Of those shot by law enforcement, 25 percent of the subjects were fleeing and 25 percent involved subjects with mental illness (more about this in our final chapter). In 75 percent of the cases, the officer was under attack or defending someone else who was under attack.

But Reyes doesn't stop there. He acknowledges that blacks are more likely to get into violent confrontations with the police (per capita), but it's because they are responsible for about 38 percent of all violent crime and 50 percent of all murders, though they represent only 13 percent of the population. He also includes his astonishing find that in the first eight months of 2016, 2,818 people were shot in Chicago. Only 12 were shot by law enforcement.

He referenced further FBI statistics showing that while blacks make up only about 15 percent of the population in the United States' largest cities, they account for 62 percent of all robberies, 57 percent of all murders and 45 percent of all assaults.

Shockingly, he adds that not only are 40 percent of cop killers black, blacks kill cops at a rate 2.5 times higher than that at which cops kill blacks.

While much of the civilian population may not know these exact numbers, they certainly know that they have been the victims of very much of that crime. And they wonder why law enforcement won't do anything about it. This my friends, is a primary complaint that many folks have against law enforcement. This is yet another reason many people dislike cops,

In perhaps one of the most profound statements this book will make, much — if not most — of the issues addressed in every chapter of this book won't be addressable until the ridiculous narratives about "race relations" are addressed.

And the first place that address needs to begin is at the administrative level of law enforcement agencies, where administrators, police chiefs, sheriffs and other politicians, have been too selfish about their own jobs to admit that false race narratives have been the worst thing that has happened to law enforcement in the last 30 years.

The timidity of both police leadership and politicians has led not only to the Ferguson Effect, but to the even more recent Pantaleo Effect, named after NYPD officer Daniel Pantaleo who was fired by commissioner James O'Neill in late Aug 2019 for his role in the unfortunate death of cigarette peddler Eric Garner.

Pantaleo Effect is said to be responsible for the dramatic decline in arrests and summonses in New York after Pantaleo's firing. Arrests dropped 27 percent and summonses dropped almost 29 percent in the week after the firing, compared to the same time period in 2018.

A retired police supervisor in Brooklyn was quoted as saying, "Of course it has to do with what happened to Pantaleo — cops are frustrated, upset. They feel they don't have the backing of downtown,

Police Headquarters and City Hall." As retired NYC police lieutenant Joe Cardinale said, "It starts with the mayor (Bill de Blasio) and all his underlings, as I call them. They just don't give them any support anymore. You can see it, morale is at an all-time low. I've never seen morale as low as it is with this administration."

Stories of departments not "watching the backs" of their own officers have become a recurring theme across the country. We shouldn't be so quick to allow the profession to blame all of its ills on "anti-cop" sentiments, when politicians and law enforcement leadership have been equally abusive to officers.

## What Cops Can Learn from Military Veterans

While some statistics while only about 6 percent of America's population serves in the military, about 13 percent of law enforcement officers are military veterans. In fact, law enforcement is the third most popular occupation for veterans, behind truck driving and management. Unfortunately, there is a wealth of talent there that law enforcement might not be exploiting.

That said, when we think military "rules of engagement," we really aren't saying anything much different than a law enforcement department's "policies and procedures." What many may not understand though is that our military's rules of engagement can change for nearly every single mission.

That means that virtually every time a unit is tasked to do something, its leader spells out what the rules will be for that mission. As a case in point, it is no secret that in the later years of the Afghanistan War, the rules of engagement became very strict.

Of course, what we're also acknowledging here is that our military members learn very early to be very flexible, and that every situation requires a different approach. We can certainly make the argument that our military operates under a much more flexible system than the very rigid top-down structure of law enforcement policies and procedures.

An intriguing point often raised when considering military veterans for law enforcement is a concern that it would be difficult to "untrain" them from habits learned that are explicitly "combat oriented." Of course, while many may not completely understand, only a very small (and I mean very small) percentage of veterans are actually "combat oriented."

The overwhelming majority of military veterans are what us military-types affectionately call "POGs" (persons other than grunts), meaning they served in "support roles." These jobs included serving as cooks, electricians, communications experts, plumbers, mechanics, etc.

Military personnel are trained in any number of job areas, with job titles and duties that correlate closely with just about any civilian job you can think of. And they are very well trained in their respective jobs.

Although – just like all law enforcement officers don't "work the streets," and while many veterans might not want you to know it – while their service to the country is greatly appreciated and honorable, only a rare few are actually trained to "kill the enemy."

Of those who were specifically trained to close with, engage and kill the enemy, they too are highly trained. And they served around the world in any number of capacities including humanitarian missions – where they would unload thousands of pounds of food and water – to starving civilians left devastated by hurricanes, floods, volcanoes, earthquakes, or even ruthless drug lords and dictators. And they would complete those missions under the most austere conditions, often having to simultaneously provide police activities in the traumatized areas.

There are actually a few pieces written suggesting that military veterans are not fit for law enforcement. The thought is a bit naïve. In fact, military veterans bring a degree of disciplined unmatched by most of the general population and are obviously not averse to training. Many have deployed around the world, are very familiar with dealing closely with other cultures and are masters at intervention and de-escalation.

That said, I think it is important in this book to address what many military veterans think and feel about — and have experienced from — law enforcement, and few have critiqued it better than Tom Ricks in his 2018 piece, "Why do so many veterans dislike police officers?," which I think will resonate with a lot of veterans.

Ricks writes that veterans feel as if cops treat them the way they think they treated Iraqis or Afghanis. Specifically, he references "with weapons, flex-ties, and shouts that often were not understood." Here, I think Ricks is very eloquently noting that some veterans are concerned about how they appeared to those people. It's actually a really great capture of the veteran's sympathetic, compassionate mind.

Another point he adds is that some veterans see that while they were engaged in taking the fight to the enemy after 9/11, local police departments were getting "militarized" with "body armor, military helmets, automatic weapons, and even wheeled armored vehicles." He writes that some veterans fear that police are not getting the training in that hardware that they received.

In one breathtaking comment on the piece, one veteran insisted that their existed a "disconnect between soldiers and police." His concern was that modern police have routinely enforced unconstitutional laws, while a prominent feature of the Soldier's Creed is to never obey an unlawful order.

Yet another voiced concern over the "militarization" of police in recent years, and what he felt was an increasing aggression by police against civilians. He too wrote that a Soldier's Creed would never allow aggression against helpless civilians at such a grand scale.

I would offer that this supports my earlier argument that police training is defective in that it places far too much emphasis on "gunmanship" and "combatives" and not enough on intervention and de-escalation.

## Police Training Needs Reform

Cops are not killing people because cops are mean people. And cops aren't killing blacks because cops are inherently racists. As we've surmised already in this book, our law enforcement officers are killing people very many times because their training is not what it should be in our age of a great understand of the physiological and psychological responses of the human body.

In my saying that, some will suggest that I'm admitting that law enforcement officers are actually killing our fellow human beings because they are trained to. Well, that's exactly what I'm saying!

I wrote in the *Preface* of this book a brief explanation of my interest in the history of combat and how it has been undertaken across the ages. Beginning as a very young U.S. Navy corpsman, "training" quickly became a very important, daily word and endeavor. In continuing my studies, I obtained a graduate degree in business, with a study focus in organizational psychology. That even further tweaked my interest in human behavior in combat, and how human beings are affected by it.

Today, there is no doubt that not only is the United States military the very best trained in the world, law enforcement officers in the United States are the best trained in the world. They are the best because much of their training is based on the same psychology as that of the military.

Very basic concepts like "360-degree security" and "complacency kills" and even "take care of the Marine to your left and right" are very recognizable in police jargon like "protect your six" and "be careful out there." More than ever, the psychology of law enforcement is steeped in a warrior's mindset.

As we've discussed, from the first day that our law enforcement officers arrive at the training academy, "combat" is ingrained into their psyche. It permeates into every fabric of their lives; from the uniforms they wear to the "back up weapon" on their ankle or inside their vest, to the tactical clip-on knife in their pocket – though quite a few wear the knife on their vest as an added show of intimidation.

The freshest recruits are shown gut-wrenching videos of officers being attacked, shot, knifed and even killed. The ultimate message in training video after training video is to show these fresh, green recruits how one of their fellow officers got killed or wounded because of his or her own complacency.

From showing officers how fast a suspect can pull a gun to the time-honored scenario of the knife-wielding suspect 20 feet away, everything is about "be ready to kill or be killed at any moment." There's even an almost religious teaching on how to re-load your weapon with your non-dominate hand in case your dominant hand and arm are severely damaged by gunfire or other combat-related injury.

Again, the basis for all training is to shoot, and shoot quickly! Never let the bad guy get the upper hand! Ever! Or you'll wind up in a training video that we'll show to rookie cops on what "not" to do.

There is no argument that a law enforcement officer is justified in using deadly force if he or she reasonably fears that a person will cause death or serious bodily harm to that officer, other officers, or to another person.

A big problem though, which many know, but few are willing to admit

– for fear of chastisement – is that almost all law enforcement training emphasizes and encourages officers to shoot if the circumstances seem "reasonable." In fact, a very large part of training encourages officers to practice being able to "articulate" why the force they used was "reasonable." Ask any law enforcement how prevalent that term "articulate" is in their training. Go ahead! I dare you!

I have emphasized several times in this book that law enforcement training overwhelming focuses on gunmanship and lacks terribly in teaching de-escalation and even simple communication skills. As a result, those officers who lack critical communications skills will naturally have a tendency to revert to their gun holsters instead of their confidence in de-escalation, because they are most comfortable using their sidearm. And as we've seen over and over again the results have been devastating.

And why wouldn't the results be devastating? The law enforcement community itself understands fully the concepts of "train like you fight" and that in the most critical moments "you will always revert back to your training."

I would offer that a major change is needed in law enforcement training to give officers the tools to allow them to not rely so heavily on their gun belt. Rather than thinking there are a plethora of bad cops out there eager for the opportunity to brutalize someone, the problem is that they are receiving inadequate training.

# POLICE MILITARIZATION

**The Soldier's Creed**
*I am an American Soldier
I am a warrior and a member of a team.
I serve the people of the United States, and live the Army Values
I will always place the mission first
I will never accept defeat
I will never quit
I will never leave a fallen comrade.
I am disciplined, physically and mentally tough, trained
and proficient in my warrior tasks and drills
I always maintain my arms, my equipment and myself
I am an expert and I am a professional
I stand ready to deploy, engage, and destroy, the enemies
of the United States of America in close combat
I am a guardian of freedom and the American way of life.
I am an American Soldier*

Part of the National Defense Authorization Act – signed into law by President Bill Clinton in 1996 – included the Law Enforcement Support Office (LESO), also known as the "1033 Program," allowed the Department of Defense to transfer excess military equipment to civilian law enforcement agencies.

In August 2014, Obama signed an executive order which resulted in the creation of the "Law Enforcement Equipment Working Group." The group issued a report recommending that the military cease transferring military equipment to local law enforcement agencies.

As Obama declared, "We've seen how militarized gear can sometimes give people a feeling like there's an occupying force as opposed to a force that's part of the community that's protecting and serving them."

President Obama would later acknowledge that military equipment had helped some law enforcement agencies during times of natural disaster, search and rescue, and even the terrorist attacks in San Bernardino in 2015 and Pulse nightclub in Orlando in 2016.

By August 2017, President Trump signed executive action which reversed the restrictions on military equipment placed by the Obama administration. Consequently, a study in the same month in *American Economic* journal specifically examined whether police acquisition of surplus military equipment actually had an effect on crime.

The study found that, as of 2014, "some 8,000 local law enforcement agencies have participated in the program resulting in more than $5.4 billion in previously purchased, surplus military gear." This gear included, "computers, air conditioners, clothing, medical supplies, flashlights, ammunition, rifles, helmets, helicopters, and armored vehicles."

It also showed that the acquisition of military equipment by a community led not only to decreases in crime, but also to a reduction in complaints about crime from citizens. That said, there has been much scrutiny about local law enforcement departments appearing more and more like military units headed to Manbij.

In 2006, the city of Baltimore began questioning the deployment of officers in its "specialized units" as it struggled to address the city's shortage of regular patrol officers. In short, the view was that the number of officers in its specialized units was way too high.

To his credit, Paul Blair – then head of the city police – asserted that the deployment of officers in units such as an "Organized Crime Division" as well as vice and narcotics units, performed duties on a city-wide level, while individual districts within the city had their own specialized units performing the same duties.

In a November 2011 issue of *The Atlantic*, Arthur Rizer – former Washington State police officer and both Purple Heart and Bronze Star recipient for action in Iraq –and Joseph Hartman – a Virginia lawyer and doctoral candidate at Georgetown University – penned a piece entitled, "How the war on terror has militarized the police."

Very critical of the militarization of police in the U.S., they suggest that newly acquired military equipment by police departments was not being used strictly to combat "terrorism" but for routine police activities.

As they proposed, while police departments had adopted military equipment, they had also adopted a "military mentality" – and by definition, military training and tactics – and that the line between "policing" and "military action" was becoming indistinguishable on American streets. In a real sense, "Special Weapons and Tactics (SWAT)" teams are no longer "special," but routine.

Many in the public see that law enforcement has moved from treating individuals as "suspects" to a mentality where even serving a simple search warrant requires a SWAT team, because individuals are no longer viewed as innocent until proven guilty. This has created a culture where law enforcement seems to possess a much more aggressive, confrontational mentality.

Let's consider that a soldier's mentality involves the acknowledgment that his or her purpose is to "destroy the enemy" of the United States. This is in stark contrast to a police officer's pledge to "protect and serve." For the average American, any attempt to merge any aspect of the two appears dangerous, even on its surface.

> *"how military personnel engage non-combatants is far more restrained and respectful than what American police often do."*

An examination of this appeared in an August 2018 piece in the online *Task and Purpose* magazine, by Jonathan Blanks – a Writer in Residence at Harvard University's Fair Punishment Project – who wrote that during his research, he found that "veterans had particular animosity or resentment for police." He insists there is good reason for this.

In what he calls the "Psuedo Militarization" of the police, Blanks research focus has been on law enforcement practices, overcriminalization and civil liberties. While he admits that he is not a military veteran, he found a surprising contrast in how military members treat non-combatants overseas compared to how law enforcement officers treat American citizens.

As he wrote, "how military personnel engage non-combatants is far more restrained and respectful than what American police often do." It is unconscionable to think that our very young military members – typically between the ages of about 18 and 22 – possess more discipline and constraint – in a foreign country, where they are at war against a foreign people who don't even speak their language – than do law enforcement officers right here at home dealing with people in their own community.

Blanks became critical of 1033 programs as he found that "departments that acquire equipment through the 1033 program have more uses of force and more fatal officer-involved shootings."

Another notable examination of police use of military equipment comes from the R Street Group – a nonprofit, nonpartisan, public policy research organization. The group's mission statement, is to, in part;

> *"work extensively on both state and national policy, and focus on issues that other groups tend to neglect. Our specialty is tackling issues that are complex, but don't necessarily grab major headlines."*

In its March 2018 review entitled, "Equip police more like Batman less like GI Joe," the group's stated purposes is to, in part, "evaluate the utility of (military) equipment for the mission of policing." The piece highlighted the group's concern for how law enforcement can accomplish its mission without "blurring the line between crime-fighter and war-fighter."

A lengthy March 2014 piece in the *The Economist* entitled, "Why America's police are becoming so militarized," also took issue with the over-militarization of law enforcement. It specifically address the idea that – while SWAT teams are clearly needed in many departments across the country to deal with "violent civil unrest and life-threatening situations" – they have in recent years been guilty of "mission creep."

It referenced a study estimating that while SWAT teams were deployed about 3,000 times in 1980, they are now deployed about 50,000 a year, most of which were not in response to violent crimes, but to raid private homes searching for illegal drugs. Other surprising examples of SWAT raids included;

- *A bar serving under-aged drinkers*
- *A barber shop (resulting in arresting 34 people for "barbering without a license')*
- *The home of a man suspected of organizing cockfights (officers used a tank which killed more than 100 birds when it rolled into the suspect's yard)*

Yet another study entitled "Militarization and police violence," appearing in the April-June 2017 issue of *Research and Politics*, asked if the militarization of law enforcement agencies lead to an increase in violent behavior among officers.

The study hypothesized that law enforcement acquisition of military equipment, by definition, required military-type training, and military training results in a military mindset. Therefore, if one is trained in military tactics and has in his possession military equipment, one will respond in a militaristic fashion, with violence and aggression.

Not surprising to many, it found, "a positive and statistically significant relationship between 1033 transfers and fatalities from officer-involved shooting across all models."

With the increased use of SWAT teams has come the controversy over what are called "no-knock raids." By no-knock raids we mean – as the name implies – that law enforcement is able to acquire a warrant to enter a home without knocking.

Typically, these raids are conducted by heavily armed and equipped SWAT teams that use battering rams, shotguns and other devices to force entry into a home or apartment with as little notice to the occupant as possible. The reasoning for the no-knock is typically justified by law enforcement out of concern that occupants might try to "flush drugs down the toilet" or may reach for weapons to engage the incoming officers.

While the issue of officer safety should absolutely be paramount, the use of these raids has been fraught with controversy, primarily because of the danger to innocents as well as officers has been notable.

A 2017 investigative report by *The New York Times* found that – from 2010 to 2016 – 81 civilians and 13 law enforcement officers across the country were killed during no-knock raids. Considering such tragic numbers of death, it should be shocking to know that in the overwhelming number of these types of raids — just as with the use of police canines — the drugs found are typically only enough to bring misdemeanor-level charges... hardly enough to put law enforcement officers or the public at such great risk.

In Wisconsin in December 2016, the Racine County Gang Unit and the FBI executed a no-knock warrant on a home while the homeowners were at work. Nothing illegal was found in the home but officers shot the family dog that ran to hide in a bedroom. A local newspaper found that — from 2010 to 2016 — Racine SWAT teams had shot and killed at least 13 dogs during such incidents.

In April 2017, Detroit officers executed a search warrant on a home while the homeowner was outside talking to her sister about a celebration they were planning for their deceased mother's birthday. Officers raided the home and shot her dog, then handcuffed the homeowner and her sister. Ultimately, they found only a small vial containing what she said was "medicinal marijuana,"

During a January 2019 raid in Houston, a search warrant was obtained because an informant reported that a couple was selling heroin out of their home. After the raid, no heroin was found, but small amounts of marijuana and cocaine were.

Initial reports were that the occupants fired on police, though it was later determined that one of the officers fired first, killing the family dog. Hearing the shots and intrusion, homeowners 59-year old Dennis Tuttle and his 58-year old wife Rhogena Nicholas fired on the officers. The homeowners and the pet were killed.

Later, controversy erupted as it was determined that the circumstances surrounding the requesting officer's request for the warrant were suspicious. About a month later, Houston Police Chief Art Acevedo admitted that the officer lied to obtain the warrant.

According to the National Canine Research Council – a group that provides online resources for police training – about half of all intentional police shootings involve dogs. Although, as the group suggests, there's never been a documented case of a dog killing an officer.

When there is an instance of a law enforcement officer killing a family pet, we might easily dismiss it as a "rare occurrences," but that would neglect the idea that many in that community would then have a reason to dislike cops. And that should cause us concern!

No-knock raids – in a country such as ours where about four out of every 10 adults possess a gun in their homes – are simply a bad idea. On its face, such tactics inevitably present a clash between law enforcement officers entering a dwelling and (rightly so) being concerned with their own physical safety and homeowners who (rightly so) feel an inalienable right to defend their own lives and property.

In the overwhelming number of cases, the (supposed) drug crime offenses that initiate such raids are not offenses which carry capital punishment (the death penalty). So, why execute a tactic which – as has been proven in so many instances – can result in the shooting or killing of a suspect without due process?

## Summation

Some studies suggest that local law enforcement agency use of surplus military equipment has resulted in a reduction of crime. Still, a wealth of information exists suggesting that the mere presence of the equipment – and certainly its overuse – can reflect negatively upon police departments.

As law enforcement agencies continue to put stock in "community policing" efforts, it seems wise to ensure that police actions do not appear to exhibit an overly aggressive use of military-acquired equipment.

Having the public see that a law enforcement agency uses that equipment in only the most extreme cases would send the very welcomed message that our law enforcement offices are indeed here to "protect and serve."

As the Heritage Foundation suggests, police departments should make effort to showcase 1033 Program equipment to the public during their community outreach events and programs, rather than having the public first introduced to the items during violent encounters.

As part of those efforts, it is important to remind both the public and the media that hardened criminals themselves are becoming more and more "militarized," resulting in it being necessary for law enforcement to stay one step ahead.

# PTSD AND LAW ENFORCEMENT

*"Be strong, saith my heart; I am a soldier; I
have seen worse sights than this"*
*— Homer, The Iliad —*

As the title of this chapter clearly suggests, we will review the mental disorder known as Post-traumatic stress disorder (PTSD). Although, you should prepare yourself now. We will review what has become a very real controversy surrounding this condition within the mental health community and at the highest ranks of the military, and we will discover how both mental health professionals and the military have done a disservice to our veterans. We will also examine how that disservice has now transferred to our first responders at home.

This chapter will include very detailed information that may be unsettling to some. I would ask that you read the information carefully and save any offense until you've read the entire chapter. Just read the information. For this author, this chapter was not a fun one to write, and I expect it won't be a fun chapter for some to read. Still, it is a perspective that needs to be told.

As with past generations, many of today's veterans have seen war, been shot at, seen their buddies killed or maimed and have deployed for months at a time. The issues of both suicide and PTSD have been extensively studied by the U.S. Department of Veterans Affairs for years. As such, it would be prudent to start there as we delve into an examination of our concerns over PTSD – and even suicide – among our law enforcement officers.

In being a member of the U.S. Navy Hospital Corps, one of our recurring mantras that both sailors and Marines would find humor in is when we'd say, "Sit down over here and let me fix you a nice warm cup of suck-it-the-fuck-up."

All good-natured ribbing of course that simultaneously sent the signal to not be a "titty baby," but that "you're with Doc now, and I'm gonna take care of you." So, that is my intent with this chapter, to fix you "a nice warm cup of suck-it-the-fuck-up."

Most have heard of the very familiar statistic that 22 veterans per day die of suicide. Studying suicide rates can be confusing as the issue can involve so many variables, but we're going to examine how the "22" number is not an accurate representation of suicide rates for our veterans.

We'll begin by using data from the U.S. Department of Veteran Affairs, Office of Mental Health and Suicide Prevention, 2016 VA National Suicide Data Report, published in Sept. 2018.

While our youngest veterans – age 18-34 – have the highest suicide rate of 45 per 100,000, veterans age 55 and over make up the majority of veterans who die by suicide at a rate of 58.1 percent. Of course, this does not at all suggest that Vietnam-era and older veterans are more prone to commit suicide than other veterans. There is simply a larger percentage of them because they outnumber other veterans.

Most striking is that the study showed the suicide rate for "never federally activated National Guard and Reserve former service members" increased from 2005 to 2015. This tells us that (at least recently) active duty service alone is not an accurate predictor of being at risk for suicide.

Further, and perhaps just as surprising, veterans who have never deployed are "more likely" to die from suicide than those who have deployed. This tells us that neither is "deployment" a sufficient predictor of suicide.

The study showed that while the total number of veterans decreased from 2005 to 2016, the average number of veteran suicides each year remained steady at a rate of about 6,000. This tells us that veteran suicides are indeed increasing slightly each year.

While the veteran suicide rate is about 21 percent higher than that of the general public, veterans have several other predictors other than military service – much less combat –that can attribute to their higher rates of suicide. Not only do males vastly outnumber females among our veterans, veterans are more likely than the general population to own a gun. Being both a male and owning a gun are predictors of being at risk for suicide, even among the civilian population.

Before we get ahead of ourselves, let's review what we know;

1. The majority of veterans who die by suicide are Vietnam-era and older Vets
2. Veterans age 18-24 have the highest rate of suicide
3. The overwhelming number of post-9/11 Vets shows no signs of PTSD
4. Suicide rates among National Guard and Reservist troops has increased in recent years
5. Troops who have not deployed are more likely to commit suicide
6. Many Vets are male and own guns

Already we see that the rate of PTSD and suicide among our veterans is an issue replete with hyperbole and myth. Add to that that many therapists still disagree on basic assumptions such as whether PTSD is a disease or a natural response to being at war.

As we move to precisely examine PTSD, we can gather very insightful information from *NIH Medline Plus*, a publication of the National Institute of Health and the friends of the National Library of Medicine. One of its online pieces entitled, "PTSD: A growing epidemic," revealed what percentage of PTSD cases each group of veterans represent;

*Vietnam veterans - 31%*
*Gulf War veterans - 10 %*
*Afghanistan veterans - 10%*
*Iraqi War veterans - 20 %*

Of course, as we've already determined above, "combat" alone is not a significant predictor of PTSD. So why then are the rates of PTSD from our most recent wars so different? Obviously, something else is going on!

In June 2017, the House Veteran Affairs Committee heard testimony regarding the Veterans Administration (VA), a part of which included an address of "fake" PTSD claims. In testimony, Dr. Harold Kudler – then acting Assistant Deputy Undersecretary for Patient Care Service at the VA – testified that while the VA provided mental health treatment for some 900,000 veterans in 2006, that number sky-rocketed to 1.6 million in 2016 (even though, as we read above, the number of veterans actually decreased during that same period). Dr. Kudlow added that the number of newer (younger) veterans seeking treatment for PTSD had doubled since 2010.

Let's review that again! While the total number of veterans decreased from 2006 to 2016, the total number seeking mental health treatment from the VA almost doubled.

Scott Faith is managing editor of *The Havok Journal*, an online journal which "seeks to serve as a Voice of the Veteran Community through a focus on current affairs and articles of interest to the public in general, and the veteran community in particular." He is a veteran of a half-dozen combat deployments and served in several different Special Operations units over the course of his Army career.

In a January 2017 piece in *The Havok Journal* entitled, "Why I'm skeptical of PTSD," Faith wrote that PTSD has become to the current generation of veterans what "back pain" was to our last generation. "Both are real conditions with real victims," he wrote, adding that both are also easily faked and hard to diagnose.

Faith makes the powerful assertion that veterans often use PTSD as a sort of "get out jail free card" or a "feel sorry for me and excuse my behavior" card. He points to the plethora of news stories where a veteran may get in trouble with the law and – very many times – either the veteran or his attorney will use PTSD as a defense. Unfortunately, as Faith so poignantly notes, few major publications are willing to be critical of these fakers.

In the few months prior to publication of this book, several headlines give a glaring view of not only how we seem to view our veterans as diseased and/or victims, but how far too many veterans themselves are guilty of screaming victimhood;

> ***Military veteran arrested at Tampa airport receiving treatment at VA hospital for PTSD***
> *ABC Action News, Tampa, Sept. 20, 2018*
>
> ***Possible link to PTSD in mass shooting leads local veteran to open up about mental struggles***
> *KSAT News San Antonio, Nov 8, 2018*

***Vet with PTSD accused of leading cops on hours-long car chase***
New York Post, Jan. 4, 2019

***Attorney: Veteran who threatened to 'shoot up' a Walmart suffers from PTSD***
The Houma Courier, Jan. 19, 2019

Chris Hernandez is a veteran of both the U.S. National Guard and the U.S. Marine Corps and served in Iraq and Afghanistan. A veteran police officer with 20 years of service, he also served as part of the United Nations police mission in Kosovo. In February 2016 he wrote a piece critical of "fake" PTSD claims in the Breach Bang Clear online magazine entitled, "Thieves and Liars; PTSD Fakers and the VA."

He boldly acknowledges what many of us veterans want to say but don't because we see how many others already view us as somehow (at least partially) mentally damaged. The issue of PTSD is one of the few issues that really gets in our craw, especially when we stand next to a scumbag who claims PTSD, and we can immediately poke holes in his stories.

Hernandez' words speak volumes;

> *"... troops coming home from deployments to peaceful countries, never hearing a shot fired, but immediately claiming PTSD. We know that in the War on Terror only a small percentage of troops actually faced an enemy, and many of those relished the experience. We have the nagging feeling most PTSD claims are more about free money than healing and recovery. Some of us have become so skeptical, we automatically throw a mental BS flag when we hear someone talk about having PTSD.'*

For both veterans and non-veterans who missed that paragraph above – and as I wrote in the chapter *Some Really Weird Stuff* – only "a small percentage" of veterans have deployed actually faced the enemy. And Hernandez recognizes that many of the veterans who actually engaged the enemy "relished the experience."

If you know a veteran who claims he or she was "in combat" and suffers because of it, do me a favor! If you didn't have him read the chapter *Some Really Weird Stuff*, have him read this one. If he or she gets defensive, chances are they're a piece of garbage!

In his writing, Hernandez noted one solider collecting VA payments for PTSD because she fell and broke her leg on the way to chow. As he wrote about such cases, "not only does it display a complete lack of honor and integrity, it also hurts a ton of people – none more so than the legitimate sufferers of PTSD."

Dr. Christopher Freuh is a professor of psychology at the University of Hawaii, who also directs research at the Menninger Clinic in Houston, Texas. He too is critical of the prevalence of "fake" PTSD claims.

Freuh spent 15 years as a psychologist serving veterans within the VA system and acknowledges that PTSD is a very real psychiatric disorder. Although, in a Sept. 2014 blog piece for *Psychology Today*, entitled, "11 reasons that combat veterans with PTSD are being harmed; Well-intentioned people are harming veterans' recovery efforts," he wrote;

> "Among those seeking PTSD services (treatment/benefits) from the VA, there are some who misrepresent or exaggerate their combat experience, some who malinger symptoms they do not have, some who exaggerate symptoms they have, some misrepresent symptoms of other psychiatric disorders as PTSD, some who do not admit to treatment benefits they experience – and some who are reporting it like it is."

Freuh argues that for many veterans, their "behaviors and recovery efforts are influenced by the contingencies the VA has set up." Clearly, he's saying that PTSD malingering by many veterans lies directly at the feet of the policies established by the VA itself. He further asserts that those VA policies have become "countertherapeutic and harmful to veterans' recovery efforts and lead to misallocation of resources."

In his work in the early 2000's, Freuh found that Vietnam-era prisoners of war (POWs) not only had very low rates of PTSD, they were actually very skeptical of PTSD claims. That Vietnam-era POWs are skeptical of PTSD claims should raise eyebrows!

Interestingly, he found that while there were only 800 Vietnam-era POWs on the VA rolls, there were over 10,000 veterans listed as suffering from PTSD because of Vietnam-era POW imprisonment.

Even more, Frueh shows that among civilian victims of psychological injury (like rape), about 50 percent show full psychological recovery, while studies show that the recovery rate for combat veterans claiming PTSD is almost zero. In fact, Freuh shows that veterans who report PTSD symptoms become increasingly worse over time until they receive 100 percent disability from the VA, "at which point an 82 percent decline in use of VA mental health service occurs."

What we're seeing here is that PTSD among veterans becomes increasingly worse until those veterans begin receiving 100 percent payments from the VA, at which time they miraculously no longer have PTSD and no longer need VA mental health services.

Again, when it comes to veterans and PTSD, something else is going on here! As Freuh surmises;

> *"The real problem is not so much veterans misrepresenting to the VA... but misrepresenting to themselves, and in the process irreparably harming their mental well-being by accepting a life as a psychiatric invalid — rather than engaged, productive members of society who have conquered their emotional troubles. The VA's*

*disability policies are well-intentioned, but they are hugely wasteful and destructive to the lives of veterans and their families."*

Freuh co-authored a seminal piece in the August 2014 issue of *National Review* with Sally Satel – also a former VA clinician and resident scholar at the American Enterprise Institute – entitled, "The other VA scandal." The article highlighted the fact that – between 2000 and 2012 – while there was actually about a 15 percent decrease in the total number of veterans, the number receiving disability compensation increased by some 50 percent.

Even more precise, the percentages of veterans from each era of service who are receiving service-connected disability pay was as follows;

11% of World War II veterans
16% of Vietnam veterans
21% of First Gulf War veterans
30% of Post-9/11 veterans

We have to ask ourselves why, as time has passed, are veterans increasingly seeking disability payments for service-connected disabilities? Is war becoming more psychologically damaging? Are veterans becoming psychologically weaker? Is it because of less stigma associated with mental health issues? What is going on?

While we would think that compensation for service-connected injuries would include things like "burns, amputations or head trauma," Freuh and Satel show that the most common claims include compensation for "tinnitus, lower-back pain, limited knee flexion, mental disorders, and scars."

As they suggest, the historic rates of veteran disability claims are due to their being able to educate themselves on social media in regard to different symptoms, as well as "social acceptance" of things like psychiatric conditions.

As they propose, imagine if doctors tell a person with a back injury that he or she will never walk again even before offering back surgery that has an extremely high success rate? In doing so, the patient would rightly think that there's no reason to waste time with surgery and physical therapy. According to Freuh and Satel, that's basically what we are doing with our veterans.

A May 2017 piece by the *Associated Press* reported that almost half of our youngest military veterans (45 percent) were seeking compensation for service-related injuries, compared to only 21 percent for Gulf War veterans of the 1990s. Even more interesting though are the comparisons of the numbers of injuries being claimed by our most recent veterans compared to older veterans;

> *WWII and Korea veterans - Only two injuries*
> *Vietnam veterans - Fewer than four injuries*
> *Our newest veterans - Eight to nine injuries*

With exaggerated media reports, tear-jerking talk-show stories and over-reaching outreach by veteran organizations, we are sending the message to veterans that they are psychologically sick and incapable of recovery. Freuh and Satel call it being "clinically irresponsible."

Many clinicians are beginning to call on their colleagues to better separate the condition of PTSD from the very separate diagnoses of depression and anxiety. I hope this book will help many to begin doing the same.

We could fill this chapter – and even the entire book – with a plethora of easily researchable articles about PTSD "fakers," and there is a growing body of scientific research addressing this phenomenon, but this is a book about law enforcement, so let's now shift to PTSD and our first responders here at home.

## Suicide and Cops

Our law enforcement officers, firefighters and front-line medical personnel very often see horrific sights of watching a severely injured person take their last breath of life, dead babies, entire families killed in traffic accidents and torn bodies. Untold numbers of horrific sights. There is much to suggest that our first responders are at greater risk of depression, PTSD and suicide than the general public.

The April 3, 2018 article in *Law Enforcement Today* magazine entitled, "Breaking out… Why I quit my job as a police officer and I'm not looking back," by Dustin Hammit, was one of many who paint a grim picture of life as a law enforcement officer.

In it Hammit says he initially enjoyed the work, but explains that the new not only wore off, it left him in despair. He describes how calls became "routine and "mundane" as he felt like most of what he was doing was dealing with "other peoples' problems" and having to "babysit adults."

Hammit's piece may remind us that it is not at all unfair to suggest that some (again, some) who enjoy policing do so because of the "fix" or "high" they get from being in a position of authority. Still, for others, the job can be emotionally taxing.

The philanthropic Ruderman Family Foundation's April 2018 "Ruderman White Paper on Mental Health and Suicide of First Responders" examined Post-traumatic stress disorder and rates of suicide among law enforcement and firefighters (to including EMTs). The group found what many of us already suspect.

It noted that law enforcement and firefighters experience PTSD and depression at rates as much as five times that of the general population. As the thinking goes, this in turn leads to higher rates of suicide. I would add that it is of particular importance for departments to recognize that both PTSD and depression can adversely affect very important decision making, not to mention overall health and fitness (of which we meticulously examined in the chapter *PTSD and Law Enforcement*).

In 2017 alone, 93 firefighters died in the line of duty, while 103 died of suicide. Among law enforcement officers, 129 died in the line of duty, and 140 died of suicide. The study added that the Firefighter Behavioral Health Alliance (FBHA) estimates that only about 40 percent of firefighter suicides are actually reported.

> ... *cops themselves kill more cops each year than gang bangers, sovereign citizens and bad domestic violence calls combined.*

Just to make sure that we're all tracking, both law enforcement and firefighters are actually at greater risk of suicide than being killed in the line of duty!

Why? Among law enforcement – and all first responders – there is often a stigma and level of secrecy about suicide, particularly within one's own department. Some say this is attributed to the machismo and "suck it up" environment of their line of work. As the thought goes, even signs of depression can be frowned upon, if not actually viewed as a sign of being "weak" in professions that value bravery, toughness and preparedness. They are responders, protectors, heroes. With that comes the expectancy of enduring hardship.

Both departments and families seldom release much information about suicides. As some suggest, suicide brings a sense of being buried "in dishonor," a concept that has long been a common taboo among warrior societies.

The general public sees law enforcement place great emphasis on in-the-line-of-duty shootings, but simultaneously sees law enforcement seemingly ignore first responder suicides. To the general public, such diametrically opposing reactions come across as insincere, if not confusing.

Sure, there is a war on cops! But cops and other first responders need to acknowledge that suicide is a bad guy too! And to make sure that we're paying attention, let's reiterate the importance of recognizing that cops kill more cops each year than gang bangers, sovereign citizens and bad domestic violence calls combined.

Either you are against first responder deaths and you want to address these tragedies, or you don't. It's time for law enforcement and other first responders to stop picking and choosing which kind of life is important.

In addressing PTSD as it relates specifically to law enforcement, a June 2017 article in *Psychology Today* called Post Traumatic Stress Injury (PTSI), "a disabling condition affecting police officers, but it's an injury, not a life sentence."

Interestingly, the author wrote;

> "These are hard times to be a cop. There are days when it seems like the actions of a few have tainted the entire law enforcement profession. Policing is a complex profession, far more complex than most people understand. What other job requires you to be combat ready at the same time you are called upon to be a counselor, a priest, a lawyer, and a social worker? What other profession authorizes you to use deadly force and then mandates that you attempt to save the person you just tried to kill?"

That simple paragraph illuminates the unfortunate reality of how we have been programmed to view our law enforcement officers. I, for one, believe it is not only unhealthy for our officers, it has been damaging to police-civilian relations.

The writer references studies that show as many as 19 percent of police officers suffer from PTSD and some 34 percent show many of the symptoms of PTSD. Accurately though, the writer acknowledges that;

> "An officer with PTSD cannot think clearly. Is probably hyper vigilant, has a short fuse, may not be sleeping well because of nightmares, might be policing in a reckless manner, constantly triggered by reminders of the event, self-medicating, or making such great efforts to avoid a similar situation that he isn't doing the job properly."

Still, while it is easy to blame stress, long hours, shift duty, missed holidays, departmental politics and a host of other "external factors" for the high rates of suicide among law enforcement, we seldom dare to consider there may be inherent "internal" factors to blame.

We know that, in many cases, becoming a police officer takes a special kind of person. We can be sure that most officers care about their communities and want to make them better. A person with a "servant's heart" who is willing to "stand the line."

So – as I've re-iterated throughout this book – what if the inherent personal psychology of that type of person makes them more sensitive to the pain and hardships of others? What if that type of person's sense of service is because they actually "feel" some things more intensely than the average person? If so, wouldn't that explain high rates of things like alcoholism and even suicide among law enforcement?

This "internal" approach of studying law enforcement psychology seems much more logical than our continually focusing on "external" forces for all of law enforcement ills. And I believe this book is one of the first works to actually give that idea serious review.

An early 2017 piece by Dr. Michelle L. Beshears entitled *Police officers face cumulative PTSD* has appeared in several police magazines.

Beshears – a psychologist who specializes in criminal justice – argues that while military members often suffer psychological injuries from a single traumatic event, "for police officers, PTSD tends to manifest over time, resulting from multiple stress-related experiences."

As she suggests, this "cumulative PTSD" is "even more dangerous" because it's more likely to go unnoticed, and there are typically no Critical Incident Stress Management (CISM) programs for the everyday small events that occur, such as;

- *long work hours*
- *handling people's attitudes*
- *waiting for the next call and not knowing what the situation will be*
- *departmental politics*

Then, on top of it all, as she writes, "officers are frequently criticized, scrutinized, and investigated for decisions they make."

Seriously! She wrote that the accumulation of those types of events can manifest into "cumulative PTSD." Give me a friggin' break!

In a piece for the *The Marshall Project* – a non-profit news organization that covers the criminal justice system – entitled, "It's time we talk about police suicide," Andy O'hara, a veteran police officer, acknowledges that more police officers die of suicide than of shootings and vehicle accidents combined. He asserts, "I believe that work-related stress and depression are far more prevalent in police work than reports suggest."

He adds too that, "while injuries like PTSD are increasingly acknowledged within the military, its prevalence in civilian police work goes virtually unnoticed." Of course, readers of this book know that for law enforcement to rely on our military's track record of dealing with PTSD is a dangerous path to travel.

While O'hara's piece is informative in many respects, I wholly dismiss his argument that PTSD among police officers should be better examined and accepted. As we have well documented in this chapter, PTSD within the military and among our veterans is seriously questionable and terribly exaggerated. And its time we let cops know that!

A March 2018 article in the online magazine *TheCrimeReport.org* entitled "PTSD: The Dirty Little Secret of Law Enforcement," also gives intriguing statistics relevant to law enforcement and PTSD. It references National Alliance on Mental Illness (NAMI) studies which show, "between seven percent and 19 percent of police officers experience symptoms of Post-traumatic stress disorder, compared to 3.5 percent of the general population."

The article does good in recognizing Maria Haberfield – political science professor at John Jay College of Criminal Justice, who also served on the Israeli National Police Force – who said, "The same way (officers) need to be qualified for firearms twice a year, it has to be mandatory to go to stress management... it needs to be institutionalized in the training."

In a very real sense, it is not so much the inadequacies or weaknesses of individual officers that has made suicide among law enforcement officers such a problem, it is the law enforcement community (meaning, the leadership) itself, because of its neglect in addressing the mental health of its officers. We can also say that PTSD has become a sort of *femme fatale* in the profession, as we're not allowed to question whether or not it really exists.

If I had one piece of advice for our law enforcement officers looking to examples of military PTSD to support the prevalence of law enforcement PTSD, I would say "Don't Do It!" Law enforcement should not allow itself to fall into the same fake PTSD trap that the many veterans have.

This has been a time bomb that has destroyed – if not grossly misdiagnosed – far too many veterans, and there is nothing worse than sending the message to our officers that they are somehow irreparably damaged, like we've done with so many of our military veterans.

We must consider that the overwhelming majority of those who join the military or serve as first responders here at home do so out of sense of "service." They naturally have that "servant's heart" that attracts them to occupations where they can serve others. We must accept that this makes these types of folks more sympathetic/empathetic when they see others perish or in pain. That itself is a predictor of depression and anxiety.

In our chapter *Some Stereotypes: Accurate and Inaccurate*, we review how some experts suggest that "police personality" may even pre-dispose officers to domestic violence. There may be an even bigger issue if we apply that recognition to suicide. What if 'police personality' – those characteristics which draw people to law enforcement careers in the first place – predispose a person to suicide? The concept is an absolute eye-opener. And I don't know if anyone has seriously raised this question.

It would make for an intriguing study to examine those with a "servant's heart" to see what factors may or may not affect their individual egos, personalities and self-esteem, and how what may or may not be a contributing factor in symptoms of PTSD and suicide.

At the beginning of this chapter, I wrote that, "this chapter was not fun to write." Now, hopefully, you see why! It seems obvious that we need a more critical – and honest – discussion of PTSD and its prevalence among our military veterans. Very many veterans are feigning PTSD symptoms for the purpose of sympathy and/or monetary gain.

With that discussion, we must ask ourselves an important question: Why was the idea of PTSD among law enforcement virtually non-existent just a few years ago but is now so centerstage that it is an integral part of law enforcement training?

Even more, in researching for this chapter, as I reached out to law enforcement officers and other first responders, I was aghast at the number of firefighters and EMTs who frantically asserted the prevalence of PTSD among their ranks. I was devastated at the idea that our first responders are so willing to claim victimhood that they blindly jump at the opportunity to identify with a condition that has already been well-documented to be over-dramatized by our veterans.

In my *Preface*, I referenced Lt. Col. Dave Grossman, former West Point Military Academy professor and favorite trainer of both the military and law enforcement. A former U.S. Army Ranger, Grossman has spent much of his career studying what he calls "killology," the study of the psychological and physiological effects of combat on humans. He insists that a pre-eminent cause of psychological injury is knowing that another human was trying to kill you or cause you great physical harm.

In short, he says that it is not trauma alone that can cause psychological injury, it is the fear of trauma being intentionally inflicted by another human being that can cause psychological injury. It is important to note that he is clear that it "can" cause injury. He does not say it "does" cause injury,

Seeing mangled bodies, dead babies or horrible vehicle accidents may cause depression and anxiety, but unlikely to cause PTSD because there was no instance of another person trying to kill you or cause you great physical harm. Anxiety? Maybe. Depression? Sure! But PTSD, unlikely. The good news – and what I hope many will carry with them after reading this book – is that depression and anxiety are very easily treated.

Many military veterans have come to realize that much of the dramatic increase of PTSD claims by their fellow veterans is not because of exposure to combat at all. It is rather simply symptoms of depression and anxiety due to the transition from life within a cohesive, well-functioning unit – where camaraderie and *esprit de corps* are high –to a seemingly boring, stale society that devalues them and their service.

This author proposes that law enforcement would do well to take this same attitude towards PTSD and recognize that it is not so much "combat" (or the fear of it) that is the greatest stressor, but rather society itself. Add to that the constant anti-cop media coverage and groups adamantly opposed to the police? There's your recipe for anxiety and depression right there!

Just as veterans suffer from lack of adequate means to "re-adjust" to civilian life, the first responder community needs to do better at not making its own ranks feel "alienated" simply because they see some bad things. Those in leadership positions introduce unnecessary stressors on their own personnel by continually reminding them (and planting a seed) that they are at high risk of PTSD, when they are simply suffering from very treatable depression and anxiety.

Much like the military, law enforcement and other first responders have been reluctant to separate the condition of PTSD from lesser diagnoses. In not separating these conditions, we're allowing our law enforcement officers, firefighters and EMTs to think they're suffering from a confusing, debilitating condition, when what they may be experiencing is easily treatable. And we can't emphasize that enough!

My message to our first responders, and to law enforcement in particular? Get the "Recognizing PTSD" programs out of your training! You're pre-conditioning our heroic brothers and sisters to feel sorry for themselves.

Another firefighter friend of mine replied to my concerns about this issue online leading up to publication of this book. His words were as follows;

> "During my career as a fireman, I spent A LOT of time away from home in fire houses. I worked 24/48 on a fulltime job and then 12 every third day on my part time job and was also a volunteer fireman. I didn't do it because of issues within my house. For me, I found it hard to turn off the fireman mindset. I didn't know how to shut it down and come home and just be a husband and dad. This routine lasted up until the last three years of my career when I realized that my family was drifting away from me. The "brotherhood" isn't as tight, for me anyways, as it's portrayed. I did have some good friend on the job and I found it easy to hang with them.... at the fire house. I was not into the bar scene due to being a little older than many in my department. My absenteeism from my family did lead to some issues within my marriage but fortunately for me, things worked out."

While suicides are self-inflicted, in-the-line-of-duty shootings are (obviously) committed by a person other than the victim. That important variable – that some other person would intentionally inflict harm on you – creates a fear that is like no other. The fear that someone else would try to "kill me."

That one variable is why we place such a higher degree of concern and fear –however rational or irrational it may be – into our discussions of officer suicide.

When we experience an officer-involved shooting, authorities remind us to wait until the investigation is final before we pass judgment on the officer involved. They remind us as well that these tragic events are indeed few and far between. By the same token, we should do the same when officers are killed in the line of duty.

As tragic as an officer death can be, we have to allow ourselves to recognize that they are indeed more rare than in some other occupations. This is absolutely not an unsympathetic position to have, especially when – as I have argued elsewhere in this book – with our current ways of dealing with officer deaths, we may well be traumatizing a profession full of officers who may are already be vulnerable to stress-related injuries.

In May 2019, even U.S. Marine Corps Commandant Gen. Robert Neller admitted that it's time to have a real conversation about PTSD proclaiming that, "there is no shame in admitting one's struggling in life."

Although, in a video posted on social media he qualified his thoughts on PTSD with very important words. He said, "Nobody said this was going to be easy, but you can deal with this. It has to be dealt with." While his message carried many more words of wisdom, these were the most powerful as they were not the "helpless victim" message we're used to.

# SOME STEREOTYPES ACCURATE AND INACCURATE

*"Never interrupt your enemy when he is making a mistake"*
*— Napoleon —*

## Female officers

*"I'd much rather be a woman than a man. Women can cry, they can wear cute clothes, and they're the first to be rescued off sinking ships"*
*— Gilda Radner, cast member of Saturday Night Live —*

As the share of female officers across the United States has grown from about 8 percent in 1987 to 12 percent by 2013, it is clear that a law enforcement culture which inherently restricts women certainly does not exist. In fact, departments across the country now actively recruit female officers.

Interestingly though, some studies show that most women who enter the law enforcement profession are either lesbian or heterosexual women who are simply more comfortable being in a male-dominated environment.

Further, reams of articles have been written on how women bring important sets of skills to today's departments. An interesting piece in the University of San Diego's *Law Enforcement and Public Safety Leadership* blog entitled "Why we need more women working in law enforcement" highlighted three key areas in which female officers have had a positive influence on the profession.

One is that female officers have proven less likely to use physical force or pull their weapon, the article suggests this is important at a time when "use of force" has come under increasing scrutiny. Some studies even suggest that female officers have been beneficial in dealing with domestic violence and sexual assault cases.

An eye-opening 2011 study in *Policing: An International Journal of Police Strategies and Management* gave great insight into the study of women serving as law enforcement officers in the United States.

Entitled "Women on patrol: An analysis of differences in officer arrest behavior," it found that while law enforcement has traditionally been associated with "hyper-masculine" traits, some homosexual men tended to engage in "impression management behaviors" and act hyper-masculine so as not to raise suspicion about their sexual identity.

This is important to consider when analyzing not only the behaviors – but also the work experiences – of female law enforcement officers. Impression management behaviors were notable when studying female officers making arrests in the presence of supervisors.

The study found that when male officers were present, female officers were *less likely* to make an arrest, but when a supervisor was present, female officers were *more likely* to make an arrest. As suggested by the *Policing* study, when male officers were present, female officers engaged in a "stereotypical feminine role… to gain acceptance and survive within the organization." On the other hand, it suggested that female officers "feel pressure to demonstrate their law enforcement competency during encounters when their supervisor is present."

In short, female officers seemed to take advantage of the situation at hand. They impress fellow male officers by allowing those male officers to make arrests, therefore ensuring their acceptance as a group member in good standing, but they exert aggressive behavior in the presence of – and to impress – supervisors.

It's interesting to consider that the law enforcement community makes great efforts to "adapt" in order to make minority communities more comfortable, but it seems to do the opposite for female officers. The profession seems to force females to adapt to the hyper-masculine culture.

While the topic of "racial profiling" may be a favorite of the media, and though it is often misused and not fairly reported, the study of arrests is certainly important for law enforcement. As noted by the *Policing* study, considering the number of police-civilian encounters, arrests are actually very rare. In fact, officers very often chose not to arrest, when they actually have good reason to arrest. Still, arrests can be a very important "gauge" used by departments to evaluate officer – and even departmental – performance.

In the spirit of the coveted "community policing" initiatives blooming across the country, many departments say that female officers bring better "nurturing" and "verbal" skills to today's modern law enforcement profession. Despite the picture these departments try paint, current studies show no differences in "nurturing" or "comforting" behaviors between male and female officers when actually dealing with the public; even with victims.

What studies do show is that the organizational culture of law enforcement work itself has more influence on officer behavior than does the officer's gender. Said another way, male and female officers conform to police rules, policies, expectations and work in very similar ways. With that being said, men and women can certainly have differing experiences in the workplace because of their gender.

An important note to that point is that within the same department there can be – at minimum – two different kinds of officers; those who enjoy taking calls so they can act out their courage, and "stations queens" who would rather take a desk job.

For female officers this can create a No-Win situation. If she doesn't engage fearlessly in calls, and actually engage in combat when called to do so, she is recognized as "just a female cop" who inherently can't perform like her male officer counterparts (who, by the way, are making the same pay as she).

If she does join in with "the fellas" in combat against violent criminals, it becomes clear very quickly that in most cases she is unable to exact the violence that her male officers generate. Very quickly, male officers might realize – and rightly so – that she "doesn't have my back." And much has been written about the idea that among many male officers, like it or not, there is a concern for officer safety. In the end, we have to consider the real perception of female officers in the eyes of male officers, and even in the eyes of the public.

My point here is to mirror findings made by the *Policing* article. Officers are going to exhibit behaviors that grant them reward from their department. Engaging in combat – within departmental policies – is a staple of law enforcement work. As the organizational culture of law enforcement generally encourages masculine behaviors, female officers will engage in those behaviors in order to be viewed positively during evaluations, promotions, etc.

The *Policing* study surmised that female officers were "more concerned than male officers" when it came to arrests, "so as to avoid appearing incompetent." It further found that female officers were "50 times more likely to arrest male suspects." While race made no difference in the decision to arrest by male officers, female officers were just over 14 percent more likely to arrest if the suspect was black. In contrast, juvenile suspects were more likely to be arrested by male officers, but less likely to be arrested by female officers.

Referencing earlier studies which suggest that "hostile demeanor" is more likely to lead to arrest, the *Policing* study proposes that males and blacks are more likely to be arrested by female officers because female officers deem their behavior to be more threatening to their safety.

This is another area that needs more study to determine if female officers are unfairly applying arrest authority, and if so, is additional training necessary? Or, is it male officers who are not applying arrest authority fairly?

A 2015 study in *Sociological Imagination: Western's Undergraduate Sociological Student Journal* entitled "Women in policing; In relation to female police officers' level of motivation toward the career, level of stress, and attitude of misconduct," examined how the "traditionally male-dominated" environment of law enforcement could create several barriers for female officers.

It found that one of the most prominent barriers women experience in law enforcement included the psychological differences between men and women, gender stereotypes and general police workplace culture. The study suggested that because female officers are forced to navigate these barriers, they experience higher levels of stress than male officers. Interestingly though, it found that female officers are less likely to engage in misconduct.

The study specifically highlighted how law enforcement agencies across the country have adjusted their inter-departmental operations to better incorporate the social experiences of Hispanics and African Americans, both in the community and within the department.

This *Sociological Imagination* study – as well as the *Policing* study we reviewed earlier – argues though that similar efforts of inclusion have not been offered to female officers. In addition, the study suggests that law enforcement agencies have not become "more feminine" with the presence of women. Rather, female officers are forced to become more masculine.

The proof may well be in that we most often hear male officers praise female officers not for exhibiting feminine traits, but rather for being "a badass."

## Glass Cliff

The *Sociological Imagination* study also found that female officers who display masculine traits are more likely to be retained and even promoted. Unfortunately, this can create what organizational psychologists call a glass cliff for women who are promoted primarily because of their gender – or maybe even certain circumstances – and not necessarily for their experience and expertise.

We should not confuse glass cliff with what has been termed "glass ceiling," which proposes that women can only reach a certain level of promotion, and no further. Glass cliff is a phenomenon which describes females being promoted for the wrong reasons, and/or at the wrong times.

The result can be that a female might find herself in a leadership position in a time of chaos and be (unintentionally) set up for failure. This can mean disaster in a profession like law enforcement, where decision making can involve life or death circumstances.

The study further suggests that – in connection with the glass cliff – females in leadership positions can often treat their female subordinates "more critically" than their male subordinates. A phenomenon the study called "Queen Bee Syndrome."

Ultimately, these women often focus not only on adopting male traits and behaviors, but on distancing themselves from other women. This becomes yet another variable disrupting efforts to incorporate female traits in a department.

One theory concerning the glass cliff is that when operations seem to be going well, the thought of specifically assigning a woman to a high-level position isn't really an issue, as the thought is more to choose "the best person for the job."

However, the suggestion is that in times of crisis there is the tendency to "do something different." That different choice can often be to place a woman in charge. In doing so, we would hope she is qualified for the position. Although, at times when things are already going bad, it presents a perfect opportunity for things to get worse.

Inevitably, we are left with a female assigned to a new position who looks like she's doing a terrible job, when actually the failures may not be of her doing at all. It might be that she was simply placed in a bad situation at a very vulnerable time.

Examples of possible glass cliff instances abound. News of females in leadership or critical positions in recent years who may well have been victims of the glass cliff are so numerous that the phenomenon is in dire need of more study. Recent examples include the following;

### 1. Abu Ghraib

*Most recall the scandal of torture and abuse of prisoners at Abu Ghraib prison in Iraq at the hands of U.S. military members in 2003. The most familiar images are those of U.S. service members forcing prisoners to "pose" while photos were taken. What many don't know is the extent to which female service members participated* in the abuse.

As male contact with a female other than one's wife was prohibited in Islam, females were used to interview and control male prisoners in order to add an additional layer of stress during prisoner interrogations.

It was later learned that female interrogators were rubbing on and "straddling" prisoners, as well as touching their genitals. One female interrogator interviewed a prisoner while she wore only a miniskirt and bra. Another removed her uniform top and began stroking her breasts. She then put her hand down her pants and, when she removed her hand, she made sure her prisoner saw that there was a red blood-like substance on her hand, which she rubbed on his face.

On one reportedly wild night of antics, female soldiers took photos while they watched an Iraqi interpreter rape a teenage boy.

Gen. Janis Karpinski was commander of Abu Ghraib prison and was the senior officer to be demoted because of the scandal. Serving as a reservist, in her civilian job she was a business consultant. In Iraq, she was placed in charge of 15 prisons and some 3.400 reservists.

She later wrote a book entitled "I was a woman in a warrior's world," outlining why she felt she was made a scapegoat.

## 2. USS Mahan

On March 24, 2014, a civilian worker with credentials to be on base gained access to the restricted area of Pier 1 of Naval Station, Norfolk, where the U.S. Navy destroyer USS Mahan was moored.

He made his way to the brow of the Mahan but was challenged by the female Petty Officer of the Watch (POOW). As he both refused her order to stop and appeared intoxicated, she drew her weapon. The intruder struggled with her and took her sidearm away from her.

Nearby was Master-at-Arms 2<sup>nd</sup> Class Mark Mayo – assigned to Naval Security Forces – who responded to the scuffle. Petty

Officer Mayo placed himself between the female POOW and the intruder and was shot several times and killed. Mayo's patrol partner — armed with a pistol — and the ship's roving patrol — armed with an M16 — engaged and killed the intruder.

Official investigation accounts blamed several layers of lax security at the base, and several naval personnel were reprimanded.

I can personally tell you that U.S. Naval personnel across the globe though were livid. The female POOW — who is in large part responsible for security of the brow of the ship — not only allowed an unauthorized person to board the ship, she allowed that intruder to take her weapon, resulting in the death of Petty Officer Mayo.

### 3. USS Fitzgerald

In 2017 the U.S. Navy destroyer USS Fitzgerald collided with a Philippine-flagged commercial ship off the coast of Japan.

In the hours preceding the collision, the commanding officer retired for the evening and Lt. j.g. Sarah Coppock took control as the Officer of the Deck (OOD). A lengthy navy investigation found several problems with leadership and operations onboard the Fitzgerald.

One of the problems though was that Coppock intentionally avoided communication that night with Lt. Natalie Combs, another female officer, who was running the ship's Combat Information Center (CIC), the ships electronic "nerve center" of the ship.

As a result of the collision, seven U.S. Navy sailors drowned.

### 4. Parkland Shooting

In the next chapter we will take a brief, but important, look at law enforcement officers in our nation's schools. For now, we'll focus on Broward County Cpt. Jan Jordan's inactions during the February 14, 2018 Parkland, Florida school shooting.

She became the Incident Commander upon arrival on the scene of this terrible incident. Rather than sending deputies into the school to kill the shooter – in accordance with departmental policy and widely accepted Active Shooter training – she ordered deputies to form a perimeter around the school, while the shooter continued killing students.

On November 15, 2018, a state commission found her ineffective leadership to be a contributing factor in the deaths of 17 and wounding of 17. She resigned five days later. For many, the fact that she remained on duty for nine months – and only resigned after the damning report – was appalling.

### 5. Brig. Gen. Brenda Carter

In June 2019, Military.com reported that Brig. Gen. Brenda Carter – the U.S. Air Force Special Operations Command's first female selected for promotion to the rank of general officer – was given a "letter of counseling" in regards to "toxic leadership" after an Inspector General (IG) investigation found that – in her previous job – she failed to treat her subordinates "with dignity and respect." She was also found to have falsified flight hours as a combat systems officer (CSO) in an attempt to receive credit – and pay – for hours of which she was not entitled.

## Female Corrections Officers

A 2014 Justice Department study found that allegations of sexual assault in prisons were rising. While we would assume that to mean prisoners assaulting other prisoners, half of the assaults reported were committed by corrections officers. Even more, we can find vast evidence showing that female corrections officers engaging in sex with inmates seems quite common.

I found several instances in my own home state of South Carolina in just the year leading up to the publication of this book. These escapades are echoed in every state across the country with embarrassing frequency.

In October 2018, a female corrections officer at Liber Corrections Institution in Dorchester, SC was arrested and charged with "criminal conspiracy, misconduct in office, first-degree sexual misconduct with an inmate, and unlawful carrying of a pistol." According to news sources, authorities also believed she conspired with an inmate to "bring contraband into the institution."

In November 2018, a female corrections officer in Richland County was arrested for having a romantic relationship with an inmate and using her home for the inmate to mail controlled substances.

In January 2019, two female corrections officers were arrested for sexual improprieties; one from Perry Correctional Institution for sending sexually explicit photos and videos to inmates, and one from Evans Correctional Institution for "first degree sexual misconduct with an inmate."

In February 2019, another female corrections officer at Lieber Correctional Institution was arrested for "engaging in a sexual act with an inmate." Authorities said that the inmate's cell phone revealed videos of the female officer having vaginal and anal sex with the inmate.

In April 2019, a female jail detention officer at South Carolina's Chester County Detention Center was arrested for misconduct in office and inappropriate contact with an inmate. It was alleged that she not only had repeated sexual conversations with an inmate but also shared information about detention center operations.

In May 2019, the South Carolina Department of Corrections Police Service issued an arrest warrant for one of its female corrections officers. She was charged with sexual misconduct with an inmate and misconduct in office after it was discovered that she had become pregnant by the inmate.

While these were just allegations at the time of publication, I hope the reader noted that all of these cases were in the same state and all within a year of the publication of this book. It is quite fair to assume that very similar cases happened in other states with the same frequency.

Maybe it's easy for male inmates to seduce female corrections officers, even though female corrections officers are clearly in positions of authority. Whatever the case, female corrections officers seem very prone to have sex on the job.

**Cops and Sexual Misconduct**

> *"We men are wretched things"*
> *— Homer, The Iliad —*

The concept of sex, infidelity and divorce is a recurring topic in any law enforcement magazine, and even in sociological studies. It's almost like law enforcement is infatuated with it. Even the titles of some of the articles seem to tell a glaring story.

Here are a few examples;

> **February 2014 in *Police One* magazine** - *"5 ways cops can 'affair-proof' their marriage"*
> **July 2015 in *Officer.com* online magazine** - *"Law enforcement & marriage: An on-going challenge"*
> **November 2015 in *Police One* magazine** - *"8 ways to repair a police marriage after an affair"*
> **September 2018 by Asst. Chief John Oldham, Jacksonville, FL Sheriff's Dept.** - *"The law enforcement marriage: Knowing when it's time to get help"*
> **November 2017 by the *Infidelity Recovery Institute*** - *"Sex, temptation, infidelity and the badge"*

In response to my asking opinions about cops and sexual misconduct on social media, here's how one woman responded. It's actually an insightful position;

> "LEO's (law enforcement officers) have a 'power' over the rest of us. I've always been respectful of all LEO's but there's also a certain 'attraction' because of their occupation and the risks they take every day. In my youth I dated a few police officers and trusting was very difficult. Women were always throwing themselves at them and they were sort of celebrities. Anyone in such a position (men or women) getting so much attention is bound to be tempted. I could never have married one. As much as I appreciate them all, I just could not have put myself in that position."

The 2015 *Police One* article (shown above) estimated that law enforcement officer marriages fail at a rate of some 75 percent, compared to an average of 50 percent among all marriages. It proposed that officers are "susceptible to extra-marital affairs" because of long work hours, working under stressful conditions, irregular shiftwork, all of which are common themes during almost any discussion of law enforcement work.

Another reason listed was what is known in the law enforcement community as "badge bunnies" and "holster sniffers." As the article suggests, these are "vulnerable or admiring members of the public eager to latch onto their very own authority figure."

I offer an alternative view though. What if, just as I proposed – that the profession may attract those who are pre-disposed to alcoholism – the "police personality" also attracts those who are pre-disposed to sexual promiscuity? Of course, I don't mean to imply that "all" law enforcement officers have some psychological deficiency or self-esteem issue which requires special attention from others.

But what if "wearing a uniform" attracts those who do? It would certainly explain why the law enforcement community itself invented the "badge bunny" moniker, and why we see that cops themselves laugh about it. Who knows?

A 2014 study by Bowling Green State University's *Criminal Justice Facility Publications*, entitled "Police sexual misconduct; A national scale study of arrested officers, gives some – not so great – news about law enforcement officers and sex on the job. The study analyzed 548 arrest cases of sworn law enforcement officers who had been arrested for sex-related crimes. Sadly, over the nine-year period of the study, law enforcement officers were arrested for rape 405 times.

Numerous studies have shown that sex-related police misconduct is actually quite common. They show that these instances very often include *quid pro quo* services for special treatment or "get out of jail free cards." Many include prostitutes, while others cite officers who take advantage of those "driving while female." Still others include "police groupies" who seek attention from law enforcement.

As the Bowling Green study revealed, almost all arrests (99.1 percent) included street-level cops or patrol officers and – most shockingly – most victims of sex-related crime involving law enforcement officers were younger than 18 years of age. I would offer that no statistic involving law enforcement is more disgusting than this one!

In the year leading up to the publication of this book, several instances of law enforcement-involved sex crimes also occurred in my own state of South Carolina. Again, these are echoed across the country, giving strong credence to the idea that there are more than just a few "bad apples" in the law enforcement profession.

In December 2018, an officer with the Marion Police Department filed a lawsuit against the Marion Police Chief claiming that he raped her several times. Her suit was for sexual harassment, sexual discrimination, retaliation, slander and defamation. According to local news sources, the Chief admits to having sexual relations with the woman. The city ultimately gave the Chief a severance package which included $35,000.

In April 2019, a Chester County deputy was arrested and charged with misconduct in office and taking bribes for allegedly promising a female that he would be lenient on her charges in exchange for both her nude photos and sex.

In June, an officer with the Landrum Police Department was charged with misconduct in office and unlawful communication for allegedly having sex on the job, which caused him to miss a police call for service.

By July, South Carolina was riveted to learn that five officers – including three who were married – and two dispatchers with the Mauldin Police Department had been engaged in a "sex ring" that had been going on for years, while the members were on duty and on city property.

In August, the Richland Country Sheriff Department arrested more than two dozen people as part of an operation targeting "both men trying to have sex with what they thought was a young girl and men involved in sex trafficking." One of those arrested was a Richland County Sheriff Deputy who "was actually on duty as a deputy for the department when he attempted to communicate with what he thought was a 15-year-old girl." Even more, he showed up to meet the girl in his patrol car, wearing his uniform.

It may even be fair to say that the idea of law enforcement sexual promiscuity is even accepted by many law enforcement supporters. And damn you if you dare raise question about it!

While writing this book, I asked on a social media page the very simple question of why issues of sex and infidelity seem to be prevalent among law enforcement. In response, a schoolteacher from Charleston, South Carolina (who I know personally) replied with the following;

*"That is very petty of you Keith Pounds. My dad was out to sea for sometimes 8 months straight protecting your behind but you didn't hear my mom saying that she didn't get enough attention and then putting marriage issues out for the public to see. You are having yourself an adult temper tantrum and a pity party. Go blow up some balloons, get a cake and have yourself a real party because this one is making you look like an immature brat! Seriously, I didn't think you were THIS immature!"*

The uncontrolled hysteria in that single paragraph is unbelievable!

## Cops and Marriage

> *"No man ever steps in the same river twice, for it's not the same river and he's not the same man"*
> *— Heraclitus —*

We're told that cops have higher divorce rates, right? And we're told that it's because of the long hours, varying shift work, the stress that officers bring home that family members have to deal with, and all sorts of other things that break up marriages. We all know that! Right? Well, there's plenty of research to prove that that's bogus!

A 2000 study by Radford University of Virginia found that law enforcement officers have "a divorce rate lower than the national average" and are actually "closer to the bottom of the list when it comes to the correlation between occupations and divorce."

Again in 2010 a study published in the *Journal of Police Criminal Psychology* (JPCP) found that the divorce rate among law enforcement was "lower than that of the general population." While the national average across all occupations was 16.96 percent, the rate for law enforcement officers was only 14.47 percent.

Even more intriguing, while we are led to believe that police shift work and stressful, dangerous environments are the cause of increased divorce rates among officers, check out these divorce rates among criminal justice occupations;

*Parking enforcement officers - 26.25%*
*Fish and game wardens - 25.53%*
*Animal control officers - 19.02%*
*Patrol officers - 15.01%*
*Detectives and police supervisors - 12.0%*
*Railroad transit police - 5.26%*

If "putting your life on the line" everyday fighting crime on the mean streets of America is so stressful that it is responsible for high rates of divorce in the law enforcement community, why is the divorce rate among parking enforcement officers almost twice the rate of patrol officers?

Why do law enforcement officers themselves believe that the rates of divorce within their profession are high? It's because they are told so in their training, that's why! And why are trainers telling cops this? They are telling their trainees this because they are told to by law enforcement administrative officials, that's why! And why are law enforcement administrative officials telling them this? Because they believe what the media says and they apparently won't do their own research, that's why!

My point here is to show that there are very many areas and topics within the professions of criminal justice and law enforcement where so-called "experts" either choose not to verify the information they're given, or they just aren't very bright, or they know that what they are telling officers is untrue, but they are telling them anyway.

I don't know the answer! What I do know is that within this singular book, I have already provided a wealth of information which should cause us to question a lot of what we have been told to believe about law enforcement. Much of the information we've reviewed so far should cause the law enforcement community to take a long, hard look at itself and stop playing "victim" on every issue with which it is confronted.

Further, we have even seen much information that should inspire our law enforcement officers, as their plight is not as bad as they have been told.

## Cops and Domestic violence

Though now a bit dated, as early as 1998, a piece by the *FBI Conference on Domestic Violence by Police Officers* sought to determine if law enforcement officers "as a group have personality characteristics that might predispose them toward domestic violence." Entitled "Is the 'police personality' predisposed to domestic violence," the paper asked if the "personality characteristics" of police officers made them "prone to a variety of inappropriate or antisocial behaviors."

To move forward though, the National Center for Women and Policing (NCWP) cites three separate studies showing that 20 – 40 percent of police families experience domestic violence. This is in stark contrast to only about 10 percent of families in the general population. According to NCWP, victims of domestic violence by an officer can often be in greater fear than other victims of this crime for several reasons;

1. The officer has a gun
2. If reported, the victim may fear that any responding officers will be colleagues of the perpetrator
3. The officer often "knows the system" and may be able to avoid prosecution

As an example, NCWP references the office of the San Diego City Attorney, which prosecuted 92 percent of referred domestic violence cases in the city, but only 24 percent of domestic violence cases involving a police officer.

The group also cites an investigation of the Los Angeles Police Department by the Office of the Inspector General finding that the punishments for officers found guilty of domestic violence "was exceedingly light." Apparently, along with high rates of alcoholism among law enforcement officers, we must also be critical about their alarming rates of domestic violence.

In May 2019, a Marion, South Carolina officer and his live-in girlfriend were both arrested for domestic violence. Both were arrested because officers couldn't figure out who was the actual aggressor.

In July 2019, a deputy with the Spartanburg County Sheriff's Office was charged with one count of second-degree domestic violence and two counts of third-degree domestic violence. He had resigned from another department about seven years prior after being charged with beating another woman. According to Spartanburg local reports, five deputies in that county had been charged with domestic violence since 2017.

Again, these are two very recent cases just from my own state of South Carolina. These too are echoed across the nation.

## Gay and Lesbian cops

A 2008 *Police Quarterly* study entitled "Gays and lesbians in law enforcement; Shared perceptions among lesbian and gay police officers," found that while departments across the country had made "great strides" in accepting gay and lesbian officers, gays and lesbians still faced barriers and even equal employment opportunities, much like women and other minorities.

A 2018 study in *Policing and Society; An International Journal of Research and Policy* gives us at least a start in reviewing the experiences of gay and lesbian law enforcement officers. Entitled "Workplace experiences of gay and lesbian criminal justice officers in the United States," it used data from a focus group of attendees of a 2012 LGBT criminal justice conference.

The study recognized that the "criminal justice culture" valued "traditional masculinity" and noted that gay male officers reported "more severe and overt discrimination experiences" while lesbian officers were said to experience "more covert discrimination."

While the *Policing and Society* study showed – as we reviewed earlier – that female officers tend to engage in "impression management behaviors" (to appear to exhibit more masculine traits), gay male officers also engaged in such behavior "so as not to raise suspicion about sexual identity."

Our point in including this information is to recognize that at least some studies show that law enforcement culture does seem to maintain a hyper-masculine identity.

## Fat Cops

For much of the 21$^{st}$ century there has been no shortage of articles about the U.S. military and its concern for the quality of candidates for recruitment into military service. At the time of writing this book, the most recent studies show that as many as 71 percent of the enlistment-age population today are unfit for recruitment in the military because of (1) lack of a high school diploma, (2) criminal records or (3) obesity.

A November 2009 piece by the Military Leadership Diversity Commission found that while the above is true for the overall U.S.

population, women and minorities are more likely than men and whites to be obese. Entitled "Requirements and the demographic profile of the eligible population," the piece found that, "female recruits, especially black women" are the most likely to be affected by the military's current weight policies. As a result, "more women than men and more racial/ethnic minorities than whites will be ineligible to enlist because of weight restrictions."

Surprisingly, it found that of the 14,000 medical disqualifications for military service in 2005, the most common reason for disqualification was "exceeding body weight/body fat limits." It quoted a 2006 National Health and Nutrition Examination Survey (NHANES) which found that among American adults, 32.2 percent were overweight, 35.1 percent were obese and 6.2 percent were extremely obese.

In 2015, the RAND corporation think tank found that one in three military-aged adults in the United States were too overweight to enlist in the military. A later 2018 RAND study of some 18,000 military personnel found that almost 66 percent of military members were either "overweight or obese." Viewing results of the study by branch of service, it found the following percentages of overweight members;

*Army - 69.4 percent*
*Coast Guard - 67.8 percent*
*Navy - 64.6 percent*
*Air Force - 63.1 percent*
*Marine Corps - 60.9 percent*

Of course, we can assume the military was using much more rigorous standards in gauging weight than many other studies. Still, the military is clearly concerned that – as obesity rates in the U.S. increase – the percentage of potential recruits for military service – particularly among women and minorities – is decreasing.

For law enforcement departments across the country, this doesn't seem to be the case at all. That is to say, the law enforcement profession in the United States has no problem outfitting even its most obese officers with a department-issued uniform to represent its profession. As a result, obesity among law enforcement officers has become one of the profession's most embarrassing eyesores.

A 2011 study by the *Journal of Emergency Mental Health* found that police officers have one of the poorest cardiovascular disease (CVD) health profiles of any occupation. It is no surprise then that other past research has found that law enforcement officers are 25 times more likely to die from weight-related disorders than from altercations with a criminal. (Recall earlier we learned that officers were also more likely to die from suicide than from an in-the-line-of-duty altercation).

Even more, in 2014, an FBI study found that a whopping 80 percent of law enforcement officers in the United States were obese. This is embarrassing when recognizing that the overall national rates of obesity were 35.5 percent for men and 35.8 percent for women.

An *American Journal of Preventive Medicine* study found that 40.7 percent of all law enforcement officers, fire fighters and security guards are obese. While this is a much smaller percentage than that found by the FBI study, it is widely acknowledged that the FBI study used much more rigorous standards.

Still, the *American Journal of Preventive Medicine* found that law enforcement, firefighters and security guards have the highest rates of obesity of all professions in the United States. Among firefighters alone, in 2014 the Centers for Disease Control (CDC) found that a whopping 70 percent were overweight or obese.

So, let's be honest! When it comes to obesity, we hear the same tired-old excuses from law enforcement that we hear on any number of other issues. It's like hearing the same story over and over, no matter the topic. They tell us that they work irregular and long hours, and are exposed to varying types of stress, resulting in poor dietary habits. Many sit stagnant in their vehicles for hours at a time, and others sit in front of a computer screen for much of the workday.

But, if this were true, why are some officers in above average physical conditioning, yet so many are… well… fat? The answer is that the law enforcement community overall is lazy, and obesity has become not only acceptable, but the obvious norm.

Here's an even better analysis though! What about the inherent dangers of law enforcement work? What about law enforcement's recurring insistence that we recognize their critical activities like chasing bad guys and encountering violent suspects?

Is officer safety important or not? The fact that obesity is nothing short of epidemic in the law enforcement profession – and among other first responders –sends the very clear message to the public that these servants, and their departments, and the profession itself, are just not as disciplined as they'd like us to believe.

The idea that these professions boast how "dangerous" the job is quickly loses traction when we see overweight, undisciplined first responders who clearly are not concerned about getting into an altercation – or any other physical activity – while on the job.

To the credit of some departments, physical fitness programs are being implemented and/or periodic physical fitness tests are required. Still, the organizational culture of others is reflected in the obesity rates of their officers. Written policy or not, if there is an organizational expectation for physical fitness among officers, it will be reflected in the appearance of officers, even if by peer pressure alone.

In the end, while the average American is not physically fit enough to join the military, he or she is more likely to be in better shape than the average cop, firefighter, EMT or security guard. This is yet another reason why many civilians have a hard time believing the argument that law enforcement's job is "dangerous." And that's another reason why many citizens dislike law enforcement.

# SOME FINAL THOUGHTS

*"People tend to be put off by the idea of selling sex, but if you spend a winter's night with one of them and talk with them about her family and so on, you're likely to find she's just like any other woman"*
— Eiji Yochikawa, The Art of War —

## Mental health and the Opioid Crisis

For law enforcement officers across the country, the ongoing mental health crisis is of serious concern. A vast number of violent police-citizen interactions can be blamed on our failure to address the mental health issues of our fellow citizens.

Much has been written about the 1970s'-era closure of mental health institutions because of fears of abuse. The unfortunate result has been that millions were left without adequate mental healthcare. It left many unable to hold down a job or even engage socially with others. As a result, we saw an explosion of Americans homeless, living on the streets.

Very many of these poor souls are violent people, and rather than being in a controlled environment where they can be cared for by mental health professionals, they are most often dealt with by law enforcement – very often after they have caused harm to others.

As those with mental health problems are unable to get adequate mental healthcare, they are also left very often to "self-medicate" with street drugs. This issue, above all others, has been the impetus of our nation's terrible opioid crisis.

An extensive September 2018 Heritage Foundation report entitled, "Policing in America," gave insight into how law enforcement officers themselves feel about dealing with the opioid crisis. According to the study, officers unanimously agreed that "the opioid epidemic is of paramount national concern" and that it "must be a top law enforcement priority."

It rightly acknowledged that dealing with America's opioid epidemic inevitably involves a range of efforts, including "prevention, intervention, and suppression." Clearly, as the opioid crisis involves a much broader picture than most realize, it is much too much for law enforcement alone to handle.

One of the most disturbing aspects of police having to deal so directly with the mentally ill is just how often those encounters can become violent, if not deadly. A July 2015 *Associated Press* piece entitled "Of all U.S. police shootings, one-quarter reportedly involved the mentally ill" says it all in its title.

The article noted that "at least 125 people with signs of mental illness" had died in encounters with the police in barely the first half of 2015. The writer made the very powerful assertion that typical tactics that law enforcement are taught to use in everyday police work are the very opposite of those which should be used when dealing with a person who suffers from a mentally illness or is in a mental health crisis.

As the writer suggested, rather than bark commands at a mentally ill person, officers should "give a lot of space, slow things down, speak calmly and not try to immediately control the situation." Unfortunately, as the article further noted, only about half of departments in the country were giving that type of training.

The article ultimately recognizes that — of course — a deadly altercation with a mentally ill person can be emotionally devastating to the officer who pulls the trigger.

Again, as overwhelming as battling drugs alone can be for law enforcement agencies, we also expect departments to deal with mental health issues, the homeless, dangerous gangs, disruptive youths, violence that is prevalent in poor neighborhoods, on top of handling routine calls.

Much like the "War on Poverty," the so-called "Drug War" is a miserable failure. Like very many social issues, it is unfair to saddle those problems on the backs of our already overloaded law enforcement agencies. Still, as we see law enforcement on the front lines in dealing with those issues, we unfairly blame them for their existence.

Law enforcement agencies in particular should work to make addressing many of those social ills the concern of politicians and bureaucracies, rather than make recurring calls for more funding to address them. That itself places the blame back on law enforcement, by their own hand.

Lastly, as part of the War on Drugs, we hear stories from across the country of law enforcement officers "passing out" because of accidental contact with fentanyl during a vehicle search. Although, as an April 2019 *Detroit Press* noted, many toxicologists are calling that narrative into question. Their position is that if one could overdose by simply absorbing the substance — even by simply by touching it — why are addicts knowingly injecting it?

The piece quotes Baltimore's Johns Hopkins Hospital medical toxicologist and emergency physician Dr. Andrew Stolbach who insists that, "drugs like fentanyl and analogs of fentanyl aren't absorbed through the skin very well at all."

As he further added, street fentanyl is "illicit fentanyl," meaning that it isn't even full strength because street dealers often "cut" the drug with heroin or other drugs. Even more is the obvious realization that common street dealers are not professional pharmacists, and certainly not chemists. These street level dealers are obviously handling the drug and not suffering from absorption of it through the skin.

In addition, the people who are actually ingesting it are also handling the drug and not suffering from a skin absorption overdose. In fact, both the American College of Medical Toxicology and the American Academy of Clinical Toxicology have reported that first responders overdosing on fentanyl from accidental skin exposure is "extremely low."

Some have suggested that the "anxiety" associated with the hype over fentanyl exposure might be a contributing factor, if not that many first responders are simply overweight and suffer from exertion during a vehicle search because they are out of shape.

If its not from "exposure" what else could it be?

## Cops and Schools

> "All men are afraid of battle. The coward is the one who lets his fear overload his sense of duty. Duty is the essence of manhood"
> – George S. Patton –

In years past, when there was a mass shooting or similar emergency, law enforcement would typically "set up a perimeter" to prevent anyone from getting in or out. Then, they would wait for a "special team" to arrive. The special team would then negotiate, enter the building, or whatever the on-scene commander dictated was the best course of action.

All that began to change after the April 1999 shooting at Columbine High School in Colorado where 12 students and a teacher were killed, and 21 others were 21 others were injured. There emerged a nationwide effort to begin training officers to immediately enter the building, "run toward the sound of gunshots" and take out the shooter. A primary reason for this was that children were precious and deserved an immediate, violent response to anyone who intended them harm.

The *Sun Sentinel* is the local paper that stood up for failed Broward County Sheriff Scott Israel, in the aftermath of the tragic February 14, 2018 shooting at Marjory Stoneman Douglas High School in Parkland, Florida. By December 2018 though, after a lengthy investigation, and in revealing what it called, "a series of blunders, bad policies, sketchy training and poor leadership," the paper changed its tune.

For many, unfortunately, the take-away from the Parkland shooting was that law enforcement's highly touted "Active Shooter" training seems not at all what they've been led to believe. And – as a result of the Parkland shooting – many now fear that the benefits of having School Resource Officers (SROs) may not only be a failure, but a lie.

The briefest of reviews of the timeline of the Parkland tragedy tells us that not only was this particular SRO unreliable, even the school staff, was ineffective in reporting the most blatant threats. Here's a timeline of some significant events that day;

> *2:19:54 p.m. Unarmed campus watchman notices the intruder and radios his observation to another watchman. He does not call a Code Red, or any other action. He is the first of three school employees who took no action.*
> *2:21:16 p.m. After receiving the call from the first campus monitor, a second campus monitor spots the intruder, but makes no calls.*

**2:21:23 p.m.** *A student notices the shooter carrying his weapon. The shooter tells the student, "You'd better get out of here. Things are gonna start getting messy." The student runs away, then informs a football coach that he saw the shooter with a gun. The coach does not call a Code Red.*

**2:21:38 p.m.** *The shooter begins firing.*

**2:22:13 p.m.** *The first 911 call.*

**2:22:51 p.m.** *Deputy Peterson and a campus monitor use a golf cart to drive to Building 12, where the shootings were happening.*

**2:23:17 p.m.** *Deputy Peterson arrives on the east side of Building 12, draws his pistol, but does not enter the building.*

**2:23:48 p.m.** *Deputy Peterson hides between Buildings 7 and 8 and radios for a nearby intersection to be blocked off.*

**2:25:38 p.m.** *Deputy Peterson radios an order to lockdown the school.*

**2:26:07 p.m.** *Four other Broward County deputies arrive at the school but hide near their vehicles.*

**2:27:03 p.m.** *Sgt. Miller arrives. There are now 8 deputies at the school, but all remain outside.*

**2:27:54 p.m.** *The shooter drops his vest and weapon and exits the school.*

**2:28:00 p.m.** *Deputy Peterson radios for officers to stay 500 feet away from the building.*

**2:29:35 p.m.** *Broward County Cpt. Jan Jordan arrives on scene, making her the most senior person on scene.*

**2:32:42 p.m.** *Four officers from Coral Springs enter the school while Broward County officers hid outside.*

**2:33:04 p.m.** *Rather than order Broward County deputies into the building, Cpt. Jordan orders officers to set up a perimeter.*

**3:11:20 p.m.** *Deputy Peterson finally departs the place where he had been hiding for over 45 minutes.*

While there are several stories of both teacher and student heroes during the Parkland shooting, at least eight Broward County deputies waited outside listening the gunshots that were killing school children. It was not just one officer who didn't react. Eight officers didn't react! It was not until the brave officers of Coral Springs arrived about 13 minutes after the shooting started that officers took action.

Cpt. Jan Jordan – who became the senior officer in charge on the scene –was said to be in a "dream-like" state, unable to give directions to responding officers. Deputy Peterson – who had served 28 years of service as an SRO – was said to have become complacent in his job. Reports of the shooting insist that after so many years serving in a school, Peterson had not been exposed to "high-risk, high-stress situations," and that inactivity and lack of experience and preparedness made him a liability during this emergency.

While the four officers of Coral Springs certainly deserve a hero's thanks, the several Broward County deputies, and even Broward County leadership, give us every reason to believe that not only are our children still very vulnerable while at school, if there is a shooting several children are going to die before law enforcement engages the shooter or shooters.

We even have reason to believe that assigning officers strictly for SRO duty – without rotating them occasionally to patrol-type positions – is a recipe for complacency and disaster.

The Parkland shooter had previously been suspended and even expelled for bringing a weapon to school. Unfortunately, he was one of thousands of students across the country who are allowed to stay in school, even though they are a recurring discipline problem.

In September 2016 he got into a fight at school and was referred to social workers rather than police. He also assaulted a student in January 2017, and, you guessed it, no police were involved.

Particularly in high schools, fights in schools are not like they were decades ago. They are weekly, if not almost daily, occurrences. While you will almost certainly go to jail for fighting anywhere else in the United States, in our public schools it is almost guaranteed that you "won't" be arrested.

School violence today is very much the fault of Obama-era policies which sought to reduce what was then labeled as the "schools to prison pipeline." Policies were implemented to eliminate certain offenses as "arrestable" so that minority students wouldn't be arrested so much. Ironically, the Parkland shooter himself had been a beneficiary of these policies as he was a discipline problem when he attended school there.

Thankfully, Trump is rolling back many of these policies. If school officials don't fight – or ignore –the effort, we may actually see some reduction in school violence, Until then, most of our public schools are very dangerous places, and, unfortunately, many – however misguided – blame law enforcement.

## Immigration

Unfortunately, the issue of immigration has become so politicized that it's difficult to discern what is really going on, or even actual numbers of illegal immigrants in the country.

Studies show that law enforcement officers themselves are divided on whether or not local law enforcement should take a prominent role in immigration.

Some suggest the reason for this is because on one hand, local law enforcement getting too involved could jeopardize community relations, especially in heavily Hispanic communities. On the other hand, local law enforcement departments are encumbered in many ways by federal regulations.

At the same time, many local departments have very important relations with federal agencies in such things as "joint task force" teams, such as a drug task force. A local department not cooperating with federal partners could risk damaging these very important relationships.

Perhaps most important though, the federal government has many "detainers" which require a local department to report or even hold an illegal immigrant suspect until federal authorities can take custody of him or her. For small departments, this can drain their very scarce resources and time.

This is a big part of why "sanctuary cities" have come to the forefront of American media. While many Americans want the federal government to deal decisively with illegal immigration, sometimes the cost of that address is put on the back of local departments who are already having a difficult time dealing with other issues.

## Prison Reform

Families across America have felt the effects of our failing prison and jail systems. Many say that the beginning of our current criminal justice system debacle began under President Clinton, who chose to "get tough on crime" by pushing for mandatory-minimum sentencing.

As Michelle Alexander – author of the book *The New Jim Crow* –wrote, "Bill Clinton presided over the largest increase in federal and state prison inmates of any president in American history."

As she further wrote;

> "By the end of Clinton's presidency, more than half of working-age African American men in many large urban areas were saddled with criminal records and subject to legalized discrimination in

*employment, housing, access to education, and basic public benefits - relegated to a permanent second-class status eerily reminiscent of Jim Crow.*

As Kelley Paul - wife of U.S. Senator Rand Paul and advocate for prison reform - said, Clinton's sentencing laws, "resulted in a 500 percent increase in the number of people behind bars in this country." Admittedly, it is not only Clinton's fault, as the so-called "War on Drugs" – strongly supported by Reagan and both Bushes – is also to blame for the increase of nonviolent offenders among our prison populations.

A December 2016 piece by The Cato Institute, entitled "Obama ignores judge's plea for justice reform," gave startling insight into our broken criminal justice system. It noted that in 1985, some 74 percent of federal criminal cases were resolved by "plea bargains." By the end of President Obama's first term, the number had increased to a whopping 97 percent.

The spike is attributed to the Department of Justice beginning to charge individuals with the most serious offense possible in order to force defendants to plea. This had the most devastating effect on low-level drug offenders, who were forced to plead guilty and received punishments "far outweighing the severity of their crimes." Those most prominently affected were African American males.

An April 2018 piece by the Heritage Foundation noted that while our federal prison system houses more than 180,000 persons, about 40,000 are released each year. As a result of what has become known as the "prison revolving door," within three years about half are re-arrested. And some studies show that about 77 percent are re-arrested within five years of release.

In recent years, "prison reform" efforts have gained traction at both the state and federal levels. Supporters of prison reform cite recent reform implemented by both Texas and Georgia, and how those efforts have reduced recidivism in those states. In the case of Texas — which began implementing serious reforms in 2005 — they've seen a 20 percent decrease in incarceration rates. To the surprise of many, Texas simultaneously saw a reduction in crime of some 30 percent.

The effort is based on the idea that helping former inmates become productive members of society — rather than continuing criminal behavior — not only helps to keep communities safe, it reduces the number of persons in prison, which is a big save for taxpayers.

Current prison reform efforts at the federal level provide for more prison programs, and even teaching parenting and relationship skills, drug and alcohol rehabilitation and job training and education. Those who participate in the programs become eligible for increased visits from family and even reduced sentences. In addition, these legislative efforts give judges more discretion in sentencing for nonviolent crimes, which would specifically address low-level drug crimes.

Along with Trump's push for prison reform, at the time of writing this book, my own state of South Carolina is working to reduce the number of nonviolent, non-sex offenders in its state prison system. A 200-page S.C. House bi-partisan support bill offers early release from prison for certain nonviolent criminals and, by removing mandatory sentences for certain crimes, gives judges more discretion in sentencing.

The legislation comes as SC prisons are experiencing growing costs of housing an increasing prison population. According to a February 2018 article in the Columbia, SC-based *The State* newspaper, South Carolina's prison population ballooned from 9,000 inmates 1983 (at a cost of $64 million) to 25,000 in 2009 (at a cost of $394 million).

As is well known, while some prisoners are clearly thugs or psychopaths with little or no empathy for others, very many find themselves in a life of crime because of external factors. These could include poor education, no jobs skills, drug or alcohol abuse, or even treatable mental health issues.

While these issues have been well-known for years, in December 2018 President Trump signed into law the FIRST STEP (Formerly Incarcerated Reenter Society Transformed Safely Transitioning Every Person) Act. The primary purpose of the law is to keep American communities safe by not only preventing inmates from committing additional crimes once they are released from prison, but to implement programs – and incentives to complete those programs –so released inmates become productive members of society.

Few can argue the fact that America's criminal justice system has been unfairly prejudiced against African American men. Most of the public – and certainly the overwhelming number of law enforcement officers –know this. But who are the boots-on-the-ground people who actually brought the millions of African American men – and men of all colors and identities – to face this unfair judicial system? The answer, of course, is law enforcement officers.

Even more are recurring reports that prisons across the country are very often failing to provide inmates protection from violence and sexual abuse within the prison. An April 2019 *Associated Press* piece highlighted a Justice Department report that the Alabama prison system was responsible for "systemic" violations. It found that the state's prisons were responsible for recurring violence, overcrowding and high suicide rates.

For every prisoner in prison, there is a mother, a father, a brother, a sister and untold numbers of other relatives and loved ones who hear the horror stories that that prisoner tells them. And who is it that the public most closely associates as causing those horror stories? You guessed it again! Law enforcement.

Again, this book is not written at all to bash law enforcement. It is intended to shed light on what much of the public sees – fairly or unfairly – in the law enforcement profession.

While the many flaws in our massive criminal justice system surely lay at the feet of lawmakers, as with so many other issues, it is law enforcement that "enforces" those flaws. This leaves a stain on law enforcement as millions of Americans have family members they feel have been unfairly treated by our criminal justice system.

That said, of all people, we would have thought that law enforcement – above all others – would have been screaming "prison reform" and subsequent efforts for programs to reduce recidivism from the rooftops. But they weren't.

It is my hope that readers will understand how the issues and concerns discussed above do well to outline why people hate cops, and what cops can do about it.

www.ingramcontent.com/pod-product-compliance
Lightning Source LLC
Chambersburg PA
CBHW051941160426
43198CB00013B/2246